BEYOND THE RAYS OF HOPE

A man's faith and attitude
amidst a terminal disease

DAVID KURT MCCLAIN

authorHOUSE®

AuthorHouse™
1663 Liberty Drive
Bloomington, IN 47403
www.authorhouse.com
Phone: 1 (800) 839-8640

Published by AuthorHouse   06/15/2016

ISBN: 978-1-5246-1258-0 (sc)
ISBN: 978-1-5246-1257-3 (e)

Dedication:

I want to dedicate <u>Beyond the Rays of Hope</u> to my family. You have been my rock and my inspiration to keep on keeping on. You are the reason that I keep on fighting even when I feel like giving up.

To my wife, Donna, I would have been gone a long time ago if it were not for you. Thank you for honoring our wedding vows, "For better or for worse, in sickness and in health...". I love ya'll.

"One Big Happy Family"
Josh, Ashley, Donna, Jeff, Kathleen, Mimi, Ben and Me

A Note of Thanks

First of all, I want to thank my Lord and Savior, Jesus Christ, for blessing me with life way beyond the ALS life expectancy.

Next, I want to thank our friend, Ann Giangarra for printing eight years of my facebook posts and my mother, Grace McClain, for the countless hours of putting this book together. Also, a thank you to my wife, Donna, for doing the proof reading of the book. Without the three of you, there would be no book.

Last, but certainly not least, I want to thank all of you who kept encouraging me to write this book. I do not want to name names for fear of leaving someone out. You know who you are and I am so grateful to each and everyone of you.

Love,
"Tex"

Foreword

This is not your typical book in that it is not written in chapter format. It is rather a (chronological) collection of my facebook posts from the past eight years (2008-2015). My eyescan computer is my only way of communicating with family, friends and the world. Each day I go on facebook to stay in touch with loved ones, friends, and those I may not even know yet. I hope when you read this book that you will be uplifted in some way.

Some of the clever "one liners" that I used in the book may seem familiar because I got some of them from my "T.V." preachers. All "HOPE" photos taken by Donna Nuzzello

Contents

Dedication: v

A Note of Thanks...vii

Foreword ix

Seasons of Our Life...2

David McClain's Letter 4

Letter To My Boys (Song)...10

Thinking Back 15

Throw-Back Thursday 18

When My Eyes Are On You 29

Kathleen's Song (Song) 31

Cheers through tears 37

His Love Of Family Triumphs 38

Ditch the "dis" and Increase the Courage 39

Fight The Fight! 44

About ALS 45

Hurricane Sandy on the Way 46

Hurricane In Your Brain?..47

Priceless! 60

Have Your Fruit and Eat it Too 60

How Long?..67

What If? 72

No Fear...74

Not Carnality But Christ...75

Now or Then?...75

Be Yoked To Jesus Or Be Choked By The World!!.................77

Armor Up And Get Your Stomp On!......................................78

Look Inside 81

Rewards To Come...85

Things That Matter 88

Quotes About Anything and Everything 93

One Day Soon 96

I Can't Imagine What to Imagine (Song)...............................97

Get Up and Try Again..104

Holiness of God...107

Apple In My Heart 111

On The Holy Spirit...112

A Few Words From My Heart.. 114

A Lesson From the Grape: 115

We Can Learn From the Eagles. 119

On Angels 120

Just Keep Climbing...121

Back or Front?...122

I Am Who I Am Because You Are Who You Are......................123

Red Hot Jawbreakers...128

Know Who Your Enemy Is!!..129

Overcomer or Overcome? 132

Cool Your Engines and Say a Little Prayer....................135

Walk in the Spirit..136

The SON That Never Sets..139

Set Goals 141

In The Furnace..142

Lesson From God and the Silversmith...........................144

Not Easy – But Worth It! 146

You Are...148

Change Friends 149

Battle With The Gnats: The Next Chapter..................... 151

Don't Fall for Satan's Placebo! 152

Need It or Want It?..155

One Prayer Away 156

Don't Sweat the Stuff..157

What If?...162

The Next Time I Speak (Song).......................................164

Just My Shell...165

Dr. Raxlen's Letter 167

Dr. Takoudes's Letter 174

Dr. Rodrigues's Letter...176

Dr. Metzger's Letter 177

Joni Eareckson Tada's Letter 178
Jason Garrett's Letter 180
Attitude 182
Ode To David With ALS... 183
When the Time is Right (Song)... 184

Seasons of Our Life:
Part One
pp. 1-22

Part Two
pp. 23-93

Part Three
pp. 94-186

Seasons of Our Life:
Part One

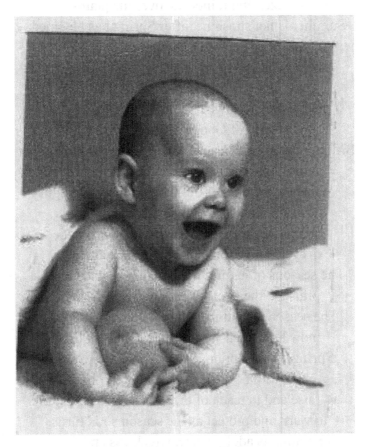

David Kurt McClain
6 months old

Seasons of Our Life

Winter, Spring, Summer and Fall, These
are the Seasons that touch us all.
Spring starts with a seed, planted and fed,
bringing new life for Summer ahead.
Flowers and showers, the smell of fresh rain, warm
breezes and rainbows, over the plains.
Summer is hot sunshine, after Spring has bloomed,
tall trees open leaves, starting in June.
Thunder and lightning and rivers that flow, green
grass and bullfrogs and fireflies that glow.
Fall is the display of Summer and Spring, the
tapestry of God, to His glory bring.
Brilliant colors and beauty which takes our breath, but
Winter is approaching, which brings forth death.
Winter is the end, of life that was new, daylight
that's dimming, and days that are few.
Winter is closure, the year is at end, but the
cycle of seasons, will soon start again.
The seasons of nature, with memories each brings,
praise to the Creator, as His creation sings.
The seasons of nature full of splendor and strife,
now let me tell you, of the seasons of life.
Spring is conception, that starts in the womb, a
child with new life, to love and to groom.
To raise and to teach of the life's lessons to learn,
to warn and protect as the season soon turns.
Summer is adolescence, wreckless and free,
circumstances of decisions, we each must see.
Decisions, careers and love in our hearts, the
love of our life and a new family starts.
Fall is mid-life, with wisdom it brings, an
empty nest, cause you cut the strings.

Long walks and cruises and warmth by the fire,
gray hair and slow life, as you look to retire.
Winter is the elderly, with smiles and with tears, the
end of life's seasons, the end of life's years.
Winter is history, with stories to tell, a good name
passed down, and knowledge as well.
The end of life's seasons, each one of us will taste, each
one will cross over, when death shall we face.
Death knows no season, it takes from all four, brings
sorrow and heartache, tears and much more.
But, no need to worry, be scared or fear, death
was defeated by One held so dear.
God sent His Son to die on a tree, He gave
up His life for He loves you and me.
So, regardless the season that you are currently in,
put your faith in Jesus and a new life begins.
By David K. McClain 6-10-12

David McClain's Letter

A Story of ALS and Hope

Greetings to each of you in the name of our Lord Jesus Christ. My name is David Kurt McClain, I was born and raised in north Texas. I came to visit the State of Connecticut back in 1984 and am still visiting. I am the husband of one and the father of three. To those who know me, I thank you for your prayers and encouraging emails. To those who don't know me, I ask that you take a moment to read this letter and consider my thoughts. I want to give each of you a quick update on my physical condition, then, I want to share something from my heart. I want to share this with you now because I don't know how much longer I have. I may have days, I may have weeks, or, God may grant me with yet another year.

I am still hanging on by a nail that God has not yet trimmed. As most of you know, I was diagnosed with Lyme disease back in 2001, then ALS (Lou Gehrig's Disease) in 2003. The average life expectancy with ALS is 1 to 3 years. I have been blessed and have beaten the average. ALS affects the brain neurons in a way so that the brain no longer communicates with the spinal cord, ultimately causing paralysis. As a result, the muscles literally "waste" away. Strangely though, ALS does not affect the mind, heart, bladder or bowels. The two main causes of death with ALS are suffocation due to lung failure and pneumonia. Currently, I am paralyzed from my shoulders down. I lay motionless for 23 of the 24 hours in each day. I am a prisoner in my own body, an alive mind in a dead shell. Imagine having your arms and legs tied up and you have an itch on your back and can't scratch it. I cannot stand, walk, sit up or move my arms and legs. My hands are swollen from lack of circulation and several times a day I have to have someone lift my arms so they won't fall asleep. Several of my toes on each foot have "curled" under. I cannot speak, eat or drink and swallowing is extremely difficult for me. I am fed by a feeding tube implanted in my stomach. I cannot breathe on my

4

own. I have a hole in my neck and a plastic tube in my windpipe from a tracheotomy that I had to have six years ago. I am on a ventilator 24 hours a day because my diaphragm muscles are too weak to fill my lungs with air. I cannot cough up the secretions in my lungs so I have a special machine that "vacuums" out my lungs. I drool uncontrollably and have a wash rag in my mouth 24 hours a day to absorb my saliva. When I get cold or stressed out, I grind my teeth and have ground much of the enamel right off of my molars. Several times a day when I either cough or sneeze, my jaw will lock up causing me to bite my tongue. I have to wait several minutes until my jaw loosens up or else I have to buzz for someone to come and pry my jaw open, releasing my tongue from the grip of my teeth. My life is lived in my mind. I lay in bed with just my thoughts and my memories. The highlight of my day is actually when I am sleeping at night. When I dream at night, I am whole, I am not paralyzed. Amazing how the mind works. It's a strange sensation that I have, in my mind, I can see my muscles moving, in my mind, I can feel my muscles moving, but in reality, nothing moves. I have a special computer that enables me to type, speak and go on the internet all with just the movement of my eyes. I am totally dependent on machines and other people just to survive each day. Little things that we take for granted like an itch on the eyebrow or mosquito landing on an arm becomes a real "nightmare" for me. Ultimately, I will either die from suffocation, or, I will die from pneumonia. I tell you the graphic details to help you understand the disease of ALS and to help you realize just how "feeble" these bodies of ours really are. I DO NOT tell you this for you to feel sorry for me... PLEASE DON'T!!!! ALS can take away many things but it CANNOT take away my attitude, my spirit and most importantly... my soul!!!!!

Now comes the good part! As I travel this journey through the "shadow of death", fear is NOT an option! My Savior and King, Jesus Christ, has carried me thus far and will continue to carry me until that day that He calls me home to Glory. The weaker that I become physically, the stronger I become spiritually because this "raggedy" old corruptible body will one day be incorruptible, this mortal will put on immortality, then, "death will be swallowed up by victory!" (1 Cor. 15:54) How awesome is that?! In this world full of hatred, sadness and despair, there is a blessed **HOPE** through Jesus Christ that heaven is a reality. Imagine a place where there will be no more tears, no more sorrows, no more crying, no more pain and no more mosquitoes!!! A place where our earthly bodies will be transformed into glorified bodies just like Jesus was when He arose from the grave. A place where we will know as we are known and where we will forever fellowship with family and friends who have gone before us. Heaven is a place where evil **CANNOT** exist, no more deception and sin. The lion will lay down with the lamb, the armadillo with the earthworm. But, above all and most importantly, Heaven is **THE** place where Jesus Christ, the very one who took upon Himself our sins and died in our place so that we can live forever and worship Him, REIGNS AS KING!!! We will live in His radiant Glory for ever and ever. The lyrics of a song written by Keith Green go something like this, "In 6 days God created the whole world, but He's been working on Heaven for 2000 years." In the book of Revelation chapter 21, we get glimpse of the Holy city, New Jerusalem, made from the purest gold and finest precious stones. There are 12 gates to the city and each one is made from a single pearl, (that's proof that the pearls came from Texas). Then, after a few more prophecy events take place on earth, we will live on a "new" earth that has been restored to perfection, just as it was before Satan messed everything up. Point being, for those of us who have trusted Christ as Savior, the best is yet to come. By the way, things get a little heated for Satan for the rest of eternity, read about it in Revelation 20:10.

Though the end of my earthly journey will bring victory and a new life with Christ, my path still has its share of "bumps". The toughest part has been preparing my wife and kids. Please pray for them, Josh (27yrs.), Ben (24yrs.), Kathleen (22yrs.) and my wife Donna (never mind age). Donna is my full time caregiver and has been by my side every step of the way. There are no words that can describe the love, gratitude and appreciation that I have for her. It brings me much comfort in knowing that each one of them has trusted their hearts to the Lord and that someday, we will be reunited again. In Christ, there are no "Good-Byes!". Looking back, I think of the things that I would do or try to achieve that would bring happiness to my life. Happiness is based on circumstances. I remember listening to an interview with Tom Brady (QB of the New England Patriots) after winning his 3rd Superbowl ring, that he still felt "empty", like, something is missing, there must be more! True happiness, joy and fulfillment doesn't come from "things" on the outside but rather, from a personal relationship with Jesus Christ on the inside. The joy of the Lord is my strength and it is that strength that gets me through each and every day. Now, my friend, I beg of you for a favor. Please look into the depths of your own heart and know that you know that you know that you are born again (John 3:1-7). Many people know "OF" Christ and think that that is good enough to get them into Heaven... Not So!! According to the Bible which is God's "love letter" written to you and to me, you must accept God's Son (Jesus Christ) as your Lord and Savior... "For God so loved the world, that He gave His only begotten Son, that whosoever will believe in Him, will not perish, but will have everlasting life". (John 3:16). If you do know Him, live for Him, love Him and let your life be a reflection of His love. If you don't know Him, realize that you are a sinner and that your sin has condemned you to eternal separation from God. Realize that Jesus Christ loves you so much that He died on the cross to free you from a literal and an eternal hell. Repent of your sins to the Lord and ask Him to forgive you. Trust your heart and your life to Him to be the Lord of your life. "If you confess with your mouth the Lord Jesus and believe in your heart that God has raised Him from the dead, you will be saved." (Romans 10:9). When that day comes for your journey to end, I will be waiting and I will rejoice with you when our Lord and Savior opens His arms and says to you "Well done, my good and faithful servant ...ENTER IN!!!"

I will close leaving you with this challenge, regardless of how high the mountains seem before you or how deep the valleys may appear, whatever the heavy weights are that pull you down or whatever the worries are that cloud your mind, know that God loves you and He knows exactly what you are going through. Give it over to Him!!!! As for me, be not upset but rejoice with me, death just brings life for eternity!! See you on the other side!

"Tex"
David Kurt McClain
January 2013

....Lord plant my feet on higher ground.

I am just a sinner saved by the grace of God.

The BIBLE ...tomorrow's newspaper.

I have been praying for several friends who have had or currently have breast cancer. I thought of Mom and jotted down these words.

Letter To My Boys

Playing in the back yard, her sons were eight and six,
looking through the window, on them her eyes were fixed.
Lord, how can I tell them, how can I explain?
Lord, please give me the words, help me through this pain.

She called them in the house that day,
and sat them on her bed,
with tears flowing down her face,
this is what she said:

CHORUS:
Boys, Mommy's gonna be leaving, Mommy's going away.
I have a home in heaven, that's where Mommy's going to stay.
Be brave, be strong, hush don't cry, Mommy loves you both so much.
I will hold you again some day, and your faces I will touch.

The treatments were so hard to take,
her strength and hair it cost.
Her faith in God was her whole life, inspite of what she lost.
A loving mother, true friend and great wife,
she never would complain,
the cancer that took her breasts, soon would take her life.

Just days before her last breath,
too weak to fight the fight,
On her mind were her two boys,
a letter she would write.
She warned them of this dark cruel world,

and the temptations they would face,
Jesus is the answer, you're covered in His grace.

She told them that their daddy,
would one day seek another,
accept her as your own,
love her, call her Mother.

Now my boys I have to go,
my time on earth is through.
I end this letter with these words,
remember that Mommy loves you!

CHORUS:
Boys, Mommy's gonna be leaving, Mommy's going away.
I have a home in heaven, that's where Mommy's going to stay.

By David K. McClain
June 21, 2010

So, thanks to our friend Adam, every person born into this world has a terminal disease, this disease is called sin. Romans 5:12 "Therefore, just as through one man (Adam) sin entered the world, and death through sin, and thus death spread to all men,"... HOWEVER, God sent the cure, His name is Jesus! Romans 6:23 ..."but the gift of God is eternal life through Jesus Christ." Accept the Cure and be healed for all eternity!

Wondering what cured ham is cured of???

Want you to know that when the winters of the seasons of your soul has you down, you'll find warmth in the blanket of God's word. What will you hear in your heart?

"....As the deer pants for the water brooks, so pants my soul for You, O God"... Psalm 42:1 ...How do you quench your thirst?

Thinking about the eagle who will fly into the storm and use its currents to rise above. What storms are you facing? Isaiah 40:31

Wants you to consider, the beauty of your fruit or the withering of your leaves is based upon how close your roots are to the rivers of water. Psalm 1:3

Just thinking: "Though we can't see the wind, we see the effects and feel the results from it. It's the same with the Holy Spirit." (Dr. Billy Graham)

..."Yesterday is history, Tomorrow is a mystery, Today is a gift from God which is why it's called "the present", live it for Him."

Saying "Thank You" to everyone. "Keep yourselves in the love of God, looking for the mercy of our Lord Jesus Christ unto eternal life."

1966
My dad (Tommy), Mom (Kathleen), me, and brother Brad

1970
My new mom, Grace, (holding Genie), Dad,
me, Brad, new sisters Kathy and Karen

Thinking Back

I was just thinking back of my upbringing in Texas and some of the "sayings" that I grew up with. I will give you a few and then make a comment or two. First... "Snug as a bug in a rug" Who thinks of these? As soon as the snug bug in the rug is spotted, it quickly becomes a casualty ....My grandmother used to tell me that I was "Warm as toast" after she would bundle me up to go outside. How long does toast really stay warm? I would have felt much better if she would have said that I was "Warm as a jalapeno stuffed microwaved burrito sprinkled with cayenne pepper." Now that, I could relate to!.... After a long days work, I would often hear "I am plum tuckered out!" Who has ever seen a tuckered plum? What does "tuckered" even mean?... When asking for directions, instead of hearing "It's over there", I would hear "It's over yonder", I never knew where yonder was much less knowing if I was over it. "Yonder", sounds like a name for a dandruff shampoo. And finally, the classic "Good night, sleep tight and don't let the bed bugs bite"! BED BUGS?!?! Now there's a comforting thought for a young child just before he goes to sleep. I remember wondering if I would wake up with a few fingers missing. They may as well told me "Good night, sleep tight and don't get hit by a train"!!!....

What a Day That Will Be

Chorus;
What a day that will be, when my Jesus I shall see,
and I look upon His face, the One who saved me by His grace;
when He takes me by the hand, and leads me through the promise land,
what a day, glorious day that will be.

Your life's journey is a process, try to enjoy every step of the way.

For You are my HOPE, oh Lord God!

All Blessing and Honor and Glory and Power are You Lord Jesus Christ.

No power from hell, no scheme of man can ever pluck me from HIS hand!!!
"In Christ Alone" by Andrew Shawn Craig and Donald A. Koch

Interview with David 1970

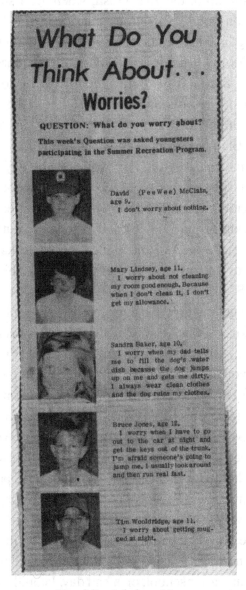

What Do You Think About...
Worries?

QUESTION: What do you worry about?

This week's Question was asked youngsters participating in the Summer Recreation Program.

David (PeeWee) McClain, age 9.
I don't worry about nothing.

Mary Lindsey, age 11.
I worry about not cleaning my room good enough. Because when I don't clean it, I don't get my allowance.

Sandra Baker, age 10.
I worry when my dad tells me to fill the dog's water dish because the dog jumps up on me and gets me dirty. I always wear clean clothes and the dog ruins my clothes.

Bruce Jones, age 12.
I worry when I have to go out to the car at night and get the keys out of the trunk. I'm afraid someone's going to jump me. I usually look around and then run real fast.

Tim Wooldridge, age 11.
I worry about getting mugged at night.

David's Advice: Now
"Worry about nothing... pray about everything!"

Throw-Back Thursday

Throw-back Thursday: This morning I was thinking back to what it was like growing up in the 70's. Gosh, where do I start? The good ole days of moon boots, eight track tapes and Starsky and Hutch. The days of big hair and mullets, I still have a mullet, but, instead of it growing ON my head, it is growing OUT my ears. I remember when I had hair, first, it turned gray, then, it turned loose. The days of Thunderbirds, Firebirds and Camaros, I was the proud owner/operator of a 1963 Volkswagen bug, I used to call her (assuming it was female) Blue Lightning, she was nothing but sheer power, 0 to 60 in ten minutes. I used in have to leave the day before just to get to school on time. Speaking of moon boots, I would have given Napoleon Dynamite a run for his money. My first eight track tape was of Three Dog Night, I don't know if today's youth even knows what an 8 track tape is. As I mentioned a few weeks ago, my first favorite song was Sugar Sugar by the Archie's. The big movie of the 70's was "JAWS", I was afraid to sit on the toilet for two weeks after I saw it. I didn't get my growth spurt until I was a sophomore in high school, my nickname was Mini Mac. Levi's blue jeans were the jeans of choice. I can still hear their commercial jingle: "Good morning world, how do you do oo oo oo oo, cause Ima wearing my Levi's, Lee E E E Lee E E E Vi's. The word "freaking" was not a word yet. See if you remember these TV series; Adam 12, Sea Hunt, Rip Cord, Rifleman, The Munsters, The Brady Bunch, Wonder Woman (cheesy, even though I had a crush on her), Six Million Dollar Man (cheesier) and The Incredible Hulk (cheesiest). Ten thousand points for each one that you remember. The days of cutting class for a bootsburger (only my Rockwall family will understand this). The days of water skiing on Lake Ray Hubbard, rafting down the Guadalupe River and taking my northern friends snipe hunting. The days of my quail hunting before and after school, on a bad day, I could shoot the knees off a bee from 60 paces, blindfolded. Ahhhh... Those were the days!!

David - (highschool)

Colossians 2:2 ..."to the knowledge of the mystery of God, both of the Father and of Christ, in whom are hidden all the treasures of wisdom and knowledge." "Knowledge and faith make a soul rich. The stronger our faith, and the warmer our love, the more will our comfort be. The treasures of wisdom are hid, not from us, but for us, in Christ." (Mathew Henry)

"Where can I go from Your spirit? Or where can I flee from Your presence? If I ascend into heaven, You are there; if I make my bed in hell, behold, You are there." Psalm 139:7, 8 ...in other words, you can run, but you cannot hide!

All things are created by Him, for Him.

Keeping the SON in His eyes!

Want folks to know that it's time to "get right" or risk "getting left"!

Wondering "If not you, who? If not now, when?"

Thinking about 1 Peter 5:10, what a reinforcement of hope!

Cast Your Care on Him

10 But the God of all grace, "who hath called us unto his eternal glory by Christ Jesus, after that ye have suffered a while, make you perfect. ¹stablish, strengthen, settle *you*.

Thinking that we, the salt of the earth, need to start seasoning!

Just thinking, if your character is built based on your word, imagine what can be built based on God's word.

Just thinking, spiritual success comes in "can's", not "cant's"!

"...Well done thou good and faithful servant, enter in..." Matthew 25:21

"BEHOLD, He is coming with clouds, and every eye shall see Him"... Revelation 1:7

"Looking at the things which are not seen, for they are eternal." 2 Cor. 4:18

Wondering if we live too much for time instead of for eternity!

One day closer, as we all are.

Giving thanks unto the Lord for He is good, for His mercy endureth forever.

David Kurt McClain

Want you to know that if you'll keep your life in tune, God will give you the song.

Suggest that you hold on loosely to the material things of this world, rather, tighten your grip on the One who died to save your soul.

Seasons of Our Life:
Part Two

Our Wedding Day: November 16, 1985

Joshua, Benjamin, Kathleen

18 years later
"Some things never change."

The next time satan reminds you of your past, REMIND HIM OF HIS FUTURE!!! Revelation 20:10 ..."The devil, who deceived them, was cast into the lake of fire and brimstone where the beast and the false prophet are. And they shall be tormented day and night forever and ever."

Your purpose in life is much bigger than yourself. You were created by God for God. What are you living for?

If Joshua and his army had stopped marching after six laps around Jericho on the 7th day, they would have lost the battle... (read Joshua chapter six for more details). What if you stop one lap shy of winning your battle?... DON'T QUIT!

Jesus never promised us that our cross wouldn't be heavy, He never promised that our hill would be easy to climb, what He did promise, is, that He would be there every step of the way!! Hebrews 13:5 ..."I will never leave you or forsake you."

Read Mark 8:22-26. Jesus spit into the blind man's eyes, when he opened his eyes he could see men as trees walking, Jesus touched his eyes and said "Look Up", when he looked and saw Jesus, he could see clearly! Turn your eyes upon Jesus and see clearly!

If you don't change your chains, your chains will change you! What are you chained to? "...For the weapons of our warfare are not carnal but mighty in God for pulling down strongholds (chains), casting down arguments and every high thing that exalts itself against the knowledge of God, bringing every thought into captivity to the obedience of Christ,"... 2 Corinthians 10:4-5 (NKJV)

So thankful that Christ doesn't leave us the way we are when we come to Him... He makes all things new!

"For lack of wood the fire goes out, and where there is no whisperer, contention quiets down. Like charcoal to hot embers and wood to fire, so is a contentious man to kindle strife... Proverbs 26:20-21 A gentle answer turns away wrath"... Proverbs 15:1 In other words, keep a cool head and chill before you spill!!

"He is the image of the invisible God, the firstborn over all creation. For by Him all things were created that are in heaven and that are on earth, visible and invisible, whether thrones or dominions or principalities or powers. ALL things were created through Him and for Him." Colossians 1:15-16 ......Just in case you are wondering "Why" you are here!

"Face to face with sin, YOU BETTER THINK AGAIN, you better think again. Take another look for a second time and give a second thought to where you draw the line!"... (Petra-Think Twice) 2 Timothy 2:22 "Flee also youthful lusts; but pursue righteousness, faith, love, peace with those who call on the Lord out of a pure heart."

Electricity enforced properly brings the blessing of light, heat and operation of machines that sustain us, on the other hand, electricity enforced IMPROPERLY can be destructive and even fatal. So are the words that come out of your mouth!

Satan's greatest weapon against you is your ignorance of the Word of God. Your greatest weapon against Satan is your knowledge of the Word of God. Are you the VICTIM or the VICTOR in your battles?

I don't need the approval of man to be who I am. I don't need this world to dictate to me how I need to look, how I need to dress or how I need to act. I was created by God, for God. I am exactly who God created me to be. I don't answer to this world, I answer to the Most High God the King of Kings the Lord of all creation. "My hope is built on nothing less than Jesus' blood and righteousness." "The Solid Rock" song by Edward Mote and William B. Bradbury

El is another name that is translated as "God" and can be used in conjunction with other words to designate various aspects of God's character. Shaddai which is derived from the word Shad meaning "breast" in Hebrew. This refers to God completely nourishing, satisfying and supplying His people with all of their needs as a mother would her child. Connected with the word for God, El, this denotes a God who freely gives nourishment and blessings. God is our sustainer.

"Shower the people you love with love,"
~~James Taylor~~

Do you tend to "wither" in the heat of the drought (Problems, Pressures and Worries)? If so, tap your roots into the LIVING WATER and go GREEN!
Jeremiah 17:7, 8 ..."Blessed is the man who trusts in the Lord, and whose hope is in the Lord, for he shall be like a tree planted by the waters, which spreads out its roots by the river, and WILL NOT fear

when heat comes; but its leaf will be GREEN, and will not be anxious in the year of drought, nor will cease from yielding fruit."

Okay, so Wednesday night, I took a brief break from the NBA playoffs and put on American Idol and happened to catch a quote by Steven Tyler... "When your face is in the sun, the shadows are behind you!" I thought about that statement in a spiritual sense ..."When your face is in the SON, the shadows are behind you!" Darkness CANNOT exist in the LIGHT... Jesus is the LIGHT of the world.

Short-term and self, or long-term and God?

When My Eyes Are On You

Lord, give me the strength to get me through,
when I am down and feeling blue.
When I'm alone and no one cares,
help me to know that You are there.
Sometimes I'm tired and feel depressed,
help me know that in You there's rest.
When times are tough and my energy's gone,
Lord pick me up and help me move on.
When I'm lonely and feeling no love,
set my eyes on You above.
Lord I thank you Lord for your life that you gave,
with me on Your mind, so I could be saved.
I love You and thank You for helping me see,
when my eyes are on You, they're not on me!

By David K. McClain
11-4-2012

Sometimes, God will take you down paths that you don't understand in order to get you where He wants you to be. If you are currently on that path, stay focused and don't lose sight of the path, your destination may not be His.

Psalm 126:5-6 ..."Those who sow in tears shall reap in joy. He who continually goes forward weeping, bearing seed for sowing, shall doubtless come again with rejoicing, bringing his sheaves with him".... In other words ...keep on keeping on sowing the GOOD seed, even though the hard times and through the tears and the blessings will be more than you can carry.

Surprise 22nd Anniversary Party

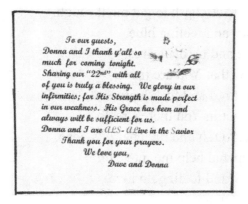

To our guests,
Donna and I thank y'all so much for coming tonight. Sharing our "22nd" with all of you is truly a blessing. We glory in our infirmities; for His Strength is made perfect in our weakness. His Grace has been and always will be sufficient for us.
Donna and I are ALS - A Live in the Savior
Thank you for your prayers.
We love you,
Dave and Donna

Celebrating our 22nd anniversary

Kathleen's Song

She blew in like a tumbleweed, Kathleen, my baby girl,
Lord help me raise her in your love, and protect her from this world.
As she grew and learned to walk, ride a bike, laugh and play,
she'd come to me with a book in hand, then I'd hear her say:

Chorus:
Daddy please read to me, I love to hear your voice,
Stories from the Bible are the stories of my choice.
Daddy please sit next to me, let me hold your hand,
Daddy don't leave me, please read to me again.

Now my little tumbleweed, has grown into a rose,
I used to call her KayKay, silly nickname I suppose.
In my mind she'll always be, Daddy's little Kay,
I can still see her great big smile, when she used to say:

Chorus:
Daddy please read to me, I love to hear your voice,
Stories from the Bible are the stories of my choice.
Daddy please sit next to me, let me hold your hand,
Daddy don't leave me, please read to me again.

I lay in bed Immovable, imprisoned in my shell,
terminally sick, I cannot speak, my days I cannot tell.
my arms and legs are paralyzed, alone throughout the day,
when she comes I wink and nod, and she can hear me say:

Chorus:
Kathleen please read to me, I love to hear your voice,
stories from the Bible, are the stories of my choice.
Kathleen please sit next to me, let me hold your hand,
Kathleen don't leave me, please read to me again.

Life is but a vapor, soon I will go home,
The Lord who is our comfort, will never leave you alone.
When your race is finished, I will greet you Kay,
We'll meet again in glory, then you'll hear me say:

Chorus:
Kathleen I will read to you, yes, you will hear my voice,
I am with the Author of the Book that is our choice.
I will sit next to you and I will hold your hand,
I will never leave you, we're in the Promised Land.

Song written by
David K. McClain
5/24/2010

My daughter Kathleen is awesome. I mean not just awesome, she is cool. She is hands down the coolest one in the house. I can't even talk about how great she is. Also, she is not prideful.

The Apple of my eye!

What if trials of this life are your mercies in disguise?

You can't outlive Him, and you can't live without Him.

James 4:14 ..."For what is your life? It is even a vapor that appears for a little time then vanishes away.": Just as a jet leaves a vapor trail in the sky for all to see, so our lives do the same. What story will your life tell when the world see's your trail.

YeeHaw!! UPS just dropped off my new Eye Max computer. I now will be able to type, talk (with a southern voice, mind you), skype, draw, paint, make phone calls, email, surf the net, turn on and off lights, TV, and my wife all with just a wink... lol, and much more. Oh, the things I used to take for granted!

Just watched "Remember The Titans" with Kathleen. Never too old to make memories!

"Even a fool is counted wise when he holds his peace"... Proverbs 17:28

"As far as east is from the west, so far has He removed our transgressions (sins) from us." Psalm 103:12 North will always meet south but east will never meet west, it travels indefinitely. So is God's love for us... Indefinite... never ending.

Just as a mirror will show the reflection of your body, the Bible will show the reflection of your spirit IF you are born again. How do you look?

Is it well with your soul?

It is encouraging to know, that at some point and time in the future, that the stand you made for Christ, and every tear you cried, and every difficult situation that you faced, and every wound you suffered in your spiritual battle, will eventually be revealed as an eternal reward.

Today, went to the hospital for routine (every ten weeks) Trach change. I get anesthesia before the procedure and I always try to see how long I can fight it before my eyes close (so far my record is .0005 seconds). When my eyes opened, I was looking at my wife's face and singing the Doxology in my mind. Someday, my eyes will close and when they open, I will be looking at my Lord and Savior's face and singing a new song. Sorry dear, as much as I love to see your face, there is another face that I have longed to see my whole life.

. _____forever

The dot (.) represents your life on earth. The line (_) represents your life in eternity...
ARE YOU LIVING FOR THE DOT OR THE LINE?

You CAN begin again!

"If you judge somebody, there is no room to love them..." (Mother Teresa)

"Death and Life are in the power of the tongue..." Proverbs 18:21 Be careful with what you say and how you say it. Your words can cut deep, the wound will heal but the scar is forever!

All the royalty of this world cannot compare to the KING OF KINGS!

I just saw an insurance ad that said that the majority of all injuries are a result from an accident. Well YEAH DUH!!! As opposed to what... on purpose???

Let the X-Ray of God's Word find your heart!

The darker it is, the brighter you should shine!

Take authority over it!!!

Pull up the loins of your mind so you don't mentally trip.

"Jesus come, release me from my demons, that I might live, in the fullness of your freedom, oh Jesus come. I will lift, my eyes upon the hill, that I might see, the One, the One who makes the water still, Jesus, make the water still." (Lyrics from "Water to Wine" Kidron Valley Psalms)

Cheers through tears

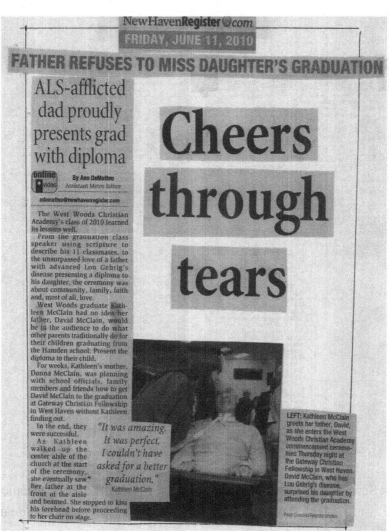

New Haven**Register** @com

FRIDAY, JUNE 11, 2010

FATHER REFUSES TO MISS DAUGHTER'S GRADUATION

ALS-afflicted dad proudly presents grad with diploma

online ▶ video
By Ann DeMatteo
Assistant Metro Editor

ademetteo@newhavenregister.com

Cheers through tears

The West Woods Christian Academy's class of 2010 learned its lessons well.

From the graduation class speaker using scripture to describe his 11 classmates, to the unsurpassed love of a father with advanced Lou Gehrig's disease presenting a diploma to his daughter, the ceremony was about community, family, faith and, most of all, love.

West Woods graduate Kathleen McClain had no idea her father, David McClain, would be in the audience to do what other parents traditionally do for their children graduating from the Hamden school: Present the diploma to their child.

For weeks, Kathleen's mother, Donna McClain, was planning with school officials, family members and friends how to get David McClain to the graduation at Gateway Christian Fellowship in West Haven without Kathleen finding out.

In the end, they were successful.

As Kathleen walked up the center aisle of the church at the start of the ceremony, she eventually saw her father at the front of the aisle and beamed. She stopped to kiss his forehead before proceeding to her chair on stage.

"It was amazing. It was perfect. I couldn't have asked for a better graduation."
Kathleen McClain

LEFT: Kathleen McClain greets her father, David, as she enters the West Woods Christian Academy commencement ceremonies Thursday night at the Gateway Christian Fellowship in West Haven. David McClain, who has Lou Gehrig's disease, surprised his daughter by attending the graduation.

Peter Casolino/Register photos

His love of family triumphs over this disease today and every day

NewHavenRegister SUNDAY, JUNE 20, 2010 **Father's Day**

His love of family triumphs over this disease today and every day

DAVID MCCLAIN is one of the strongest people I know. And, I'd like to nominate him for Father of the Year.

Despite being trapped in a body that no longer allows him to walk, chew or speak, David, 48, is still fully engaged in life.

And, he knows more than anybody that, when the Lord says it's time, he will depart this life a happy man.

ANN DEMATTEO
INSPIRATIONS

"I have a peace inside me that the Lord has given me. I'm in a win-win situation, whether I live or die. The best is yet to come for me," David told me when I visited his New Haven home last week.

online Read the story and see the video of David McClain participating in his daughter's graduation video at West Woods Christian Academy at http://www.nhregister.com/articles/2010/06/15/aa1_hamden_graduation061510.txt.

How could a man who has suffered so much from amyotrophic lateral sclerosis — Lou Gehrig's disease — have such a positive attitude?

"I rely on my faith to fuel my attitude," said David.

And he says his faith comes from the personal relationship he has built with Jesus Christ since he was a boy growing up in Texas.

When David was 6, his father, Tommy McClain, showed him the Bible and how to give his life to Jesus. Shortly thereafter, his mother died of cancer when she was 30. In a letter to her family before she died, she asked that Tommy find a "Godly woman" to raise David and his brother, Brad. That woman

David McClain of New Haven, who suffers from Lou Gehrig's disease, says faith in the Lord and family sustains him.

Peter Casolino/Register file

was Grace Scoville of Connecticut, who moved to Texas with her two girls after a mutual friend suggested she and Tommy meet. Later, when David was 24, Tommy and Grace Scoville moved to Connecticut, and David came along.

David joined Heritage Baptist Church in Wallingford and was in the choir.

One day in May 1985, a girl from Hamden who happened to be from my neighborhood, Donna Mazelka, visited the church. As soon as David saw Donna, he whispered to the guy next to him that Donna was the girl he was to marry. Fifteen days later, he proposed.

Donna and David's love story is as much about the Lord as it is about themselves and their three children: Joshua, Ben and Kathleen. It is a story I just have to tell you about.

I first learned of David's courage and spirit two weeks ago when I was preparing to cover the June 10 graduation of West Woods Christian

See DeMatteo, C2

Continued from C1

Academy in Hamden. Donna and the folks at school had kept secret from Kathleen that her dad was attending her graduation. The last time he was out of the house was in October, to go to church. Everyone was thrilled to see David, especially Kathleen.

There was not enough room in that story to describe how David lives his life with advanced ALS, so I thought I would tell you more today. Please watch the video attached to this story online. It shows how David uses his eye-scan computer, which has a little camera. The clicking you hear is when his eye meets the letters on the computer screen to type the words he is thinking. Then, his eye meets another button, and a computerized voice pronounces the thought. The eye-scan computer was a donation from Voices for Joanie, named after a woman who died from ALS.

"Faith and love in God is the foundation of love for my wife, family and friends," says David.

David was diagnosed in 2003 after he started slurring his words. At about the same time, he was bitten by a tick and was treated for Lyme disease. Donna said that he took some natural drugs, things she believes have sustained him.

Prior to his illness, David had worked for Connecticut Steel in Wallingford, and Donna taught fifth-grade at West Woods Christian Academy. She is now his full-time caregiver.

Two days after their 22nd anniversary in November 2007, David suffered from double pneumonia. Doctors convinced him to have a tracheotomy so it would be easier to control his secretions. "We knew the ALS was getting worse," Donna said.

Said David, "No disease or handicap can steal away my love. I've had a lot of time to think and reflect on what is really important in life. It's relationships with God, family and friends."

Post Script: In 2013 Ann passed away after losing the battle to cancer. She was a talented reporter and a friend who will be missed dearly by all those who knew her.

Ditch the "dis" and Increase the Courage

Been feeling discouraged lately? Maybe some bad news has your feeling blue? Having problems with a relationship or perhaps, a certain decision didn't go your way? The reasons for discouragement can sometimes seem endless. Let's break it down and nip it in the bud. Start by thinking what it is that is discouraging you. There are a couple main areas to explore. First area, between the ears. As Zig Ziglar, (famous motivational speaker) used to say, "You got to get rid of that Stinkin Thinkin!", if you don't, then you will need a "Check Up From The Neck Up!" You've heard it said that "Attitude is Everything", well, I happen to believe this is true. You can be discouraged or encouraged simply by how you perceive the situation you're in. This world can be a very negative place to hang out at times, especially if your focus is more on the horizontal than on the Vertical. Romans 12:2 says, ..."and do not be conformed to this world, but be TRANSFORMED by the renewing of your mind" (no stinkin thinkin), "that you may prove what is that good and acceptable and perfect will of God." You see, being discouraged is nowhere in God's plan and will for your life. Now, let's take a look at the word "discouraged" itself. What is the foundation of this word? Yep, you guessed it... COURAGE! What is courage you ask? I always thought that courage was bravely leading the troops into battle or being the first one to try your sister-in-law's new recipe for corn pudding, but, it goes beyond that. Courage is the ability to confront fear, pain, danger, uncertainty, intimidation and corn pudding. Not just the ability to confront, but the confidence to confront as well. Where do we get confidence? According to Proverbs 3:26 ...The Lord! Therefore, it is the Lord who gives us the confidence to confront ANYTHING that stands to "dis" our courage. Courage comes from the heart. I'm not talking about that ticking organ that sits inside of your chest, I'm talking about that deep, deep feeling that you get inside, that gut feeling. Psalm 27:14 tells us to "Wait on the Lord, be of good courage and He will strengthen your heart." The word "Wait" can have two applications. The first application is patience, waiting on God as He speaks to you through prayer and studying God's word. The second application is likened to that of a waiter who "waits" on you in a restaurant. His job is to serve you and to do as you ask. This is our very purpose, to serve God and do what he asks, WAIT UPON THE LORD. In other words, if we are patient, strive to serve and obey God, then, He promises to give us the strength to face ANY challenge that tries to discourage us. Will there be trials and tribulations in our life? Absolutely! Is God aware of what we are going through, He does promise us this, IF we put our faith and trust in Jesus, IT WILL BE WORTH IT!! God will allow trials to enter our lives, not because He wants to be mean and watch us suffer, but, because He loves us and He wants to teach us to rely SOLEY upon Him to carry us through them. As a matter of fact, in the book of James, chapter one (I highly recommend that you read this chapter the first chance you get), we are instructed to count it joy when we encounter various trials. Say WHAT? Be happy during times of trials? HOW? You have to first realize that your problems aren't your problems, they belong to the Lord, so, give them to Him. The joy of the Lord is our strength, get into the Word of God and you gain inner strength that you never knew existed. As a body builder endures the temporary burn and pain while lifting, the end results is increased size and strength. The same applies to spiritual body building, we will experience temporary burning and pain in this life, but, curl the Word and watch your spiritual size and strength increase beyond limits. To sum it all up, here's a new one for ya, LET GO AND LET GOD! How many times have we heard that but refuse to heed its wisdom? It's time to ditch the "dis" and increase the courage. Defeat defeat, live encouraged!!!

(DKM)

"The Great Creator is ALSO my Savior!"

"When the world says you can't, FAITH says you can!!!"... (Kutless ...That's what faith can do)

Don't let this world change your character, rather, let your character change this world!

I am under the influence of FAITH!!!!

When in doubt.... Go fishing!

Taking the test of time ...hoping I pass!!!

Run from darkness into the SON!!!

Instead of begging the rocks to fall on you when it is too late (Revelation 6:15, 16) ...fall on the ROCK while you still have a chance

"Dear God, may your Spirit stomp out the flames of my flesh".

Want a blessing from God? Pray for Israel.
Genesis 12:3 NKJV "I will bless those who bless you (Israel), and I will curse him who curses you;"

..."Here am I; send me".

Live like there's nothing to fear ....there isn't!!! 2 Timothy 1.7

10/10/12   Josh, Ben, Kathleen and proud Dad

Can I take just a moment to brag a little bit? I have the greatest kids and future daughter-in-laws in the world!!! I am so proud of each of them that I can't stand it! Each one loves the Lord which is the most important thing a person can do!

This weekend, Josh will be competing in the United Illuminating's lineman rodeo which will be held in Kansas. The competition consists of fastest times climbing up and down a utility pole, rescuing a 180 pound dummy from the top of the pole and several other daring feats. Let em have it Josh and let em know that there is a McClain out there! I love you!

My son Ben will be performing with the Extreme Impact team this weekend. He is one of eight guys who will be doing amazing feats of strength such as breaking bricks set on fire, breaking baseball bats and 2X4's like they were toothpicks, ripping phone books and metal license plates in half, blowing up hot water balloons up until they burst and loads of other wild and crazy things. After the show, the guys will share their testimony. Get after it Ben and let em know there's a McClain out there! I love you!!

And then there's the apple of my eye, Kathleen. She is a junior at Nyack College and has a full scholarship in softball, she was chosen by her coach to be a captain because of her leadership abilities and positive attitude. She is also an RA in her dorm and is a tremendous witness and mentor to the girls on her floor and on her team. Kathleen, get after it and let 'em know that there is a McClain's out there! I love you!!!

Finally, Ashley and Mimi, my two future daughter-in-laws. Are you sure ya'll want to join this crazy family? Let 'em know that there are two future McClain's out there!! I love you both so dearly!!

The past is the past, let it go. What matters now is... where you go from here.

Matthew 6:33 KJV "But seek ye first the kingdom of God, and His righteousness; and all these things shall be added unto you."

Fight The Fight!

You would never fight a physical battle without the knowledge of your enemy and the proper weapons. The same should apply when you are fighting spiritual battles.

Ephesians 6:10-18 NKJV "Finally, my brethren, be strong in the Lord and in the power of His might. Put on the whole armor of God that you may be able to stand against the wiles of the devil. For we do not wrestle against flesh and blood, but against principalities, against powers, against the rulers of the darkness of this age, against spiritual hosts of wickedness in heavenly places. Therefore take up the whole armor of God that you may be able to withstand in the evil day, and having done, all, to stand.
Stand therefore, having girded your waist with truth, having put on the breastplate of righteousness, and having shod your feet with the preparation of the gospel of peace; above all, taking the shield of faith with which you will be able to quench all the fiery darts of the wicked one. And take the helmet of salvation, and take the sword of the Spirit, which is the word of God; praying always with all prayer and supplication in the Spirit, being watchful to this end with all perseverance and supplication for all the saints."

There may be pain in the night, but, joy comes in the morning.

2 Corinthians 4:17 KJV "For our light affliction, which is but for a moment, work's for us a far more exceeding and eternal weight of glory."

About ALS

The two main causes of death for ALS victims are pneumonia and respiratory failure. I have a machine called a cough assist. It fills my lungs up with air, then, it quickly sucks the air out pulling out the junk and the secretions, it is literally a vacuum cleaner for my lungs. So, pneumonia aint happening. Because I am on a ventilator, respiratory failure aint happening. The only way that respiratory failure would be an issue, would be, if Donna unplugs me, that is why I try to stay on her good side... LOL. Statistics told me that I had 3 to 5 years to live, here I am 12 years later, still kicking (figuratively... LOL) I don't live by statistics, I live by the grace of God, someone needs to tell statistics about the grace of God. I have been told by doctors that I can live a long long time on the ventilator, now, I am more concerned that I will never die... LOL. ALS has NOTHING on me.

Luke 9:13, 14 ...When the disciples expressed concern about where the crowd of thousands would eat, Jesus offered a surprising solution: "You feed them." The disciples had focused their attention on what they didn't have--food and money. Do you think that God would ask you to do something that together you and He couldn't handle? (Tindale).

Hurricane Sandy on the Way

10-28-12

Hunkering down for Hurricane Sandy, gonna be an interesting few days ahead!!!

10/29/12

Change of plans, I will be going to the hospital to wait the storm out. This will be the best thing for both my family and me. Pray for Connecticut!!!

10/31/12

I want to thank all ya'll who took a moment and said a prayer for the safety for my family and myself during Hurricane Sandy. I was taken to the hospital to ride the storm out just in case we lost power. We only lost a couple of trees and some siding on the front of our house. We did not lose power. This was a devastating storm for the coastlines of New Jersey, New York and Connecticut as I'm sure you've seen on the news. Though our section of town was barely touched, homes on the shoreline 20 minutes away were completely washed away in the Long Island Sound ...total destruction in portions of these 3 states. Please continue to pray for those who lost everything. Thanks again for your love and prayers!!!

Hurricane In Your Brain?

Does your mind ever get so clogged up with the "stresses" of life that you can't even think straight anymore? Do you wonder if you're coming or going? Have you ever felt like you just can't take it anymore and wanted to throw in the towel? Does it feel like you have a hurricane in your brain? Recently, I was reading about the Category 5 hurricane Katrina that slammed into New Orleans, Louisiana and parts of Mississippi back in August of 2005. I am not sure what the highest category there is for hurricanes, but, a Category 5 can carry wind speeds of up to 175 miles per hour, it's a monster!! The satellite view of Hurricane Katrina showed it to be as large as the state of Texas, and believe me, that's large! By the time she hit Louisiana and Mississippi, she had downgraded to a Category 3 with wind speeds of 125mph, which is still a very dangerous and deadly storm. Katrina caused 81.2 billion dollars in damage, 1,832 deaths and flooded over 80 percent of New Orleans. The winds and floods brought TOTAL destruction to many areas. Having a hurricane in your brain can bring TOTAL destruction to certain areas of your life such as your attitude, relationships with others and your testimony, just to name a few. You see, Katrina didn't start off as a Category 5 hurricane, it started as a breeze. By the time it hit the Bahamas, it had grown into a tropical depression. Under certain "situations" (water temperature, air temperature etc.) it quickly turned into a tropical storm. As more "situations" were added to the storm, the pressure became stronger and stronger and it soon reached a Category 1 hurricane, then, more "situations" and suddenly a Category 2, then 3, then 4 and finally Category 5. It's the same with your brain. A hurricane in your mind starts with just a "breeze", then, "situations" happen and the breeze becomes a depression. Add more "situations" and now you have a storm brewing. More "situations" on top of the "situations" and soon you have a full blown 'cane in the brain.' Now, here's the good news, UNLIKE a hurricane that develops in the ocean that we cannot control, we CAN control the storms that develop in our mind. HOW? The simple answer can be found in the gospel of Mark 4:35-40. Here, we have the account of Jesus and His disciples crossing the Sea of Galilee after having a bible study with the multitudes. Suddenly, a mighty storm came out of nowhere, the winds picked up and the waves started tossing their boat around like a leaf in the wind. The high waves were crashing the boat so hard that it was filling with water and the disciples were afraid the boat was going to sink and were fearing for their lives. Now, what I find interesting here is this, we know that at least 4 of the 12 disciples were fishermen and spent most of their lives fishing the Sea of Galilee; they knew this Sea very well. For them to be fearing for their lives, I am assuming that the winds were of hurricane force. Anyway, the answer to their storm and the answer to your storms was and is within arm's reach. The disciples looked to Jesus for deliverance. Calmly, Jesus looked at the storm and said "PEACE, BE STILL", and IMMEDIATELY the waves calmed down and the winds stopped blowing and the sea became smooth as glass. Point being, the very same Jesus who calmed the storm on that sea is the very same Jesus who can calm the storms that cloud your mind. Could Jesus have calmed the storm before the disciples came to Him? Why did He wait? Jesus wanted His disciples to know that it is HE who they should look to in the midst of the storm. In the same manner, Jesus wants YOU to know that it is HE who you should look to in the midst of your storms. When you feel like your mind is being tossed like a leaf in the wind, look to Jesus and listen for His gentle voice to say "PEACE, BE STILL" and feel the calmness come over you. Look to the Creator of the winds to calm the hurricane in your brain!!! (DKM)

Bring me joy, bring me peace, bring the chance to be free, bring me anything that brings You glory. And I know there'll be days when this life brings me pain, but if that's what it takes to praise You, Jesus, bring the rain... (Mercy Me; Bring the Rain)

All to thee, my blessed Savior... I surrender ALL
Just to be in Your presence Lord... I give You my everything!

...When I think of where I'm going, in terms of where I've been, it makes me glad to know my Lod, that I've been born again...

The life I'm living is not my own.

The true test of the strength of a tree will occur in the midst of the storm. The taproot of an oak tree can grow as deep as the tree is tall with its lateral roots branching off the taproot as wide as the branches as above the ground. Just like the oak tree, the true test of the strength of a person occurs during his or her storms of life. Your strength is determined on how deep that you are tapped in the word of GOD. God never promised that this life would be a problem and trial free, however, He DOES promise to give us the strength to get through the storms IF we truly trust in Him.

ALL storms will end!

"Keep your eyes straight on the path, do not look to the left or the right... remove your foot from the evil" Proverbs 4

You don't have to see the whole staircase, all that you really need to see is the first step. Psalm 37:23 "The steps of a man are established by the Lord..." What are you waiting for?

David Kurt McClain

We have enough youth, how about a fountain of "smart"!

For every turbulent storm, there is a sure foundation!

Not only should we think about Jesus Himself and speak about Him and believe in Him, but we should come to the point that the disciples had arrived at in Luke 24:31,... "and they KNEW Him."

Instead of thinking about who you aren't, focus on who you are! Choose one area of your life that you may be weak in and strive to strengthen that area. Reach out to someone who is going through a tough time. Pray for and with them.

What is ANYTHING to the God who created EVERYTHING? "Seek ye first the kingdom of God..." Matthew 6:33

Money isn't everything, but is sure keeps the kids in touch!

"The ways of a man are before the eyes of the Lord...." Proverbs Chapters .....You can run but, you cannot hide.

No seed will grow without the sun... No seed will grow without the SON.

"A soft answer turns away wrath..." Proverbs 15:1

If you get into Gods Word... Gods Word will get into you.

When you squeeze a wet sponge, what comes out is what it was soaking in. The same is true with you..... soak in the WORD.

The Truth is a person... His name is Jesus... find Jesus and you will find the Truth.

The human brain: The left side ...there's nothing right. The right side ...there's nothing left.

Hey, that's my girl!

Nyack College Softball – Kathleen

Congrats senior infielder Kathleen McClain from Nyack Softball, who was the female recipient of the Harold W. Bowman Character Achievement Award! #WarriorBanquet2014

Well, she did it!!! My baby girl and apple of my eye is graduating college tomorrow. I am so excited and am so very proud of her that I could dance a jig. Congrats KayKay, your hard work has paid off. I LOVE YOU!

God is our heavenly Father, or, "Daddy" if you will, He wants that close of a relationship with us. He wants to fellowship with us, He wants to dine with us, He wants to hear from us every day, and He wants to answer your prayers if you will only ask Him. God's name is Holy. Jesus laid the foundation on how to pray when He gave the sermon on the mount' (Mathew 6:9-13), "Our Father who art in heaven, hallowed (Holy) be Thy name"... Any time we speak His name, it should out of praise and adoration. Instead of from our brains to our lips, it should be from our heart to our lips.

Don't get so caught up in and with the creation that it overshadows the CREATOR.

IF... Jesus Christ is NOT your Lord and Savior ...Be Afraid ...BE VERY AFRAID!!!

Need Prayer??? Message Me... I have plenty of time on my hands.

Instead of worrying on the things that 'might' be, focus on the things that are!

It must be something in the water over here... within 6 months, all 3 of my kids got engaged. Josh and Ashley back in August, Ben and Mimi back in November and Kathleen and Jeff ...last night! Gonna be a busy and fun year.

You cannot change your past, however, you CAN change your future!

The wisdom of this world is foolishness to God. Where do you seek wisdom?

"Therefore, if anyone is in Christ, he is a new creation, old things have PASSED AWAY, behold, all things have become new." 2 Cor. 5:17
Since the old things are PASSED AWAY, isn't it time to bury them?

Poor isn't being without a dollar, poor is being without a dream!!

Give a cup of water in the name of the Lord!

Jesus will take your burden but you need to let it go.

11/8/13

My WINNING Team

Jeff, Kathleen, Josh, Ashley, Ben, Mimi & Me

Getting ready for my oldest son, Josh, wedding on the beach. I am the best man ...gonna be a fun evening!!

Ashley and Josh catching air.

On their Wedding day, August 29, 2013

We can see who will wear the boots in this new family!!

My oldest son Josh, is a lineman for the United Illuminated Company. Tomorrow, he will be competing in the UI rodeo held in Kansas City. Instead of bulls and horses, he will be facing a 75 foot utility pole. He will compete against lineman from all over the country, several events, fastest time up and down the pole, rescuing a 160 pound dummy, no, it's not me, from the top of the pole and a mystery event.

Josh.... BE SAFE, HAVE FUN and most important ...LET 'EM KNOW THAT THERE IS A McCLAIN IN THE COMPETITION.

This race CAN be won!

Ben and Mimi's Wedding day, June 21, 2013

<u>Ben & Mimi McClain Photos</u>

I had the great pleasure of capturing one of the most important days for this special couple. We started at First Baptist Church in Wallingford for their vintage inspired engagement shoot. This is the same place we ended up on June 21, 2013 for their wedding! There was no shortage of interesting...
DANIELLEMARTINE.SHOOTPROOF.COM

Rolling down the aisle

Kathleen and Jeff's Wedding day
May 24, 2014

Priceless!

Katheen and David on her Wedding day.
5-24-14

Have Your Fruit and Eat it Too

Galatians 5:22-23 NKJV "But the FRUIT of Spirit is love, joy, peace, long suffering (patience), kindness, goodness, faithfulness, gentleness and self-control."

Notice how it says fruit (singular) and not fruits (plural). Also, notice that the first adjective mentioned is love. What or who is love? 1 John 4:7, 8 ..."For love is of God... For God is love..." If you have Love (Jesus), then, you automatically have joy, peace, patience, kindness, goodness, faithfulness, gentleness and self-control. It is a package deal. If you have Jesus, you have these traits, what you do with them is up to you. It's like you can have your cake and eat it too, or should I say "You can have your fruit and eat it too."

Gravity is gravity whether you believe it or not ...Jesus Christ is the King of Kings and Lord of Lords whether you believe it or not.

You are bound to the consequences of your decisions ...good or bad.

Think before you say it' ...Think before you act on it.

Time doesn't heal your pain.... God does.

If you are praying for someone... don't give up.

PRAYER IS THE ANSWER

Sin is a cancer!!!
Not my will, but, THY will be done.

"And when I'm doing well, help me to never seek a crown, for my reward is giving glory to You..." ...Keith Green

Okay you prayer warriors, I need your help, tomorrow, my daughter, Kathleen is getting married and there is a chance of thunderstorms. Join me and let's pray the storms away.

I want to take a moment to thank all of you prayer warriors who join me and prayed the thunderstorms away yesterday. It was a beautiful day.

David Kurt McClain

Never think that your prayers are ineffective.

Cold is not the opposite of heat, it is the absence of heat. Darkness is not the opposite of light, it is the absence of light. Evil is not the opposite of good, it is the absence of good. Hate is not the opposite of love, it is the absence of love. Death is not the opposite of life, it is the absence of life. Put your faith and trust in Jesus and He will fill the absence in your heart.

"THE HEAVENS DECLARE THE GLORY OF GOD!!" Scientist now believe that there are 300 Sextillion stars, that's 300,000,000,000,000,000,000,000,000 in case you're counting. Psalm 147:4 He (God) tells the number of stars; He calls them all by their name. Imagine that! And you thought you had alot to remember! God even knows the number of hairs on your head. Not much to remember when it comes to my head!!

Do not allow situations and circumstances that surround you to weaken who you are on the inside, rather, allow Jesus to use those situations and circumstances to strengthen who you are on the inside. Romans 8:37 "Yet in all these things" (problems) "we are more than conquerors through Him who loves us."

It will be worth the wait!
John Waller – "While I'm Waiting"
Youtube.Com

Jesus: Where all hope, peace and joy are found.
"Come One, Come All" - Youtube.Com

God's name is El Elyon

The Most High God

El is another name that is translated as "God" and can be used in conjunction with other words to designate various aspects of God's character. Elyon literally means "Most High". It expresses the extreme sovereignty and majesty of God and His highest preeminence. When the two names are combined -- El Elyon -- it can be translated as "the most high exalted God".

Psalm 57:2

Another step forward towards our final destination - A New Temple Training Center is being built in Jerusalem - Prophecy Today Video Update

It is said that the shepherd will "break" the leg of the sheep who keeps wandering away, then, the shepherd will carry the sheep until its leg mends. Once mended, the sheep never leaves its master's side. The word of God "breaks" us from bad habits and sinful lifestyles as Christ carries us through. Once mended, will you stay or stray? 1 Peter 2:25

What if God hadn't sent His Son, as Savior of this earth, there'd be no cross, no empty tomb, there'd be no virgin birth. BUT, God loves this world so much, He DID send His own Son, His reason was to give the gift of salvation to everyone. So, as this season brings you gifts, and presents that you love, let's not forget the greatest gift, given from God above.

Our very existence is a gift from God. Every breath we take, every beat of our heart is the count down to our last. Life is too short to harbor grudges, resentment and bitterness, it's time to cast those aside. Never miss the opportunity to tell somebody that you love them. Don't wait until tomorrow, tomorrow may never come. Love is the only gift that lasts forever. JOHN 3:16

"Thy word is a lamp unto my feet and a light unto my path"... Psalm 119:105. Since Jesus (the WORD) is the lamp and the Spirit is the oil, there is an infinite supply of light to direct us down the path of life. If you constantly stumble off the path, hold tightly to the lamp, keep it before you and stumble no more!

A seed must die completely before it can be planted and bear its fruit, likewise, we must die completely to ourselves before God can plant us and we bear His fruit... 1 Peter 2:24

Psalm 147:4 "He counts the number of stars; He knows them all by name." "Since God created and knows each star by name, imagine how much He loves you... are you not greater than the stars? "He searched the depths of our heart and loves us the same"... Chris Tomlin (Indescribable)

"I will rise when He calls my name, no more sorrow, no more pain. I will rise on eagles wings, before my God, fall on my knees"... Chris Tomlin (I will Rise) When God calls, will you hear His voice?

Treasures of this earth are temporary, but, treasures in heaven are eternal; where are the treasures of your heart? "Do not lay up treasures on earth, where moth and rust destroy and where thieves break in and steal; but lay up for yourself treasures in heaven"... Matthew 6:19-20

When God's word is abandoned, Satan fills the void. Stay in the Word and there will be no void!

"THANK YOU" to everyone who reminded me that I am one year older. At my age, I look forward to A.M. and BM!! Seriously though, "THANK YOU" to all of you prayer warriors for "praying" me through another year. Each day is a gift from God and I am truly grateful for the life that God has blessed me with. Please keep praying and "who knows" maybe I will reach the "half century" mark next March.

My greatest need is His greatest deed... The Cross! "Turn your eyes upon Jesus, look full in His wonderful face, and the things of earth will grow strangely dim, in the light of His glory and grace". "Turn You Eyes Upon Jesus" Song by Helen H. Lemmel

When the world says "You can't", FAITH says "You can". Seek the Creator of faith and overcome the world. Galatians 2:20 "I have been crucified with Christ; it is no longer I who live, but Christ lives in me; and the life which I now live in the flesh I live by FAITH in the Son of God who loved me and gave Himself for me."

Elisha his servant, surrounded by the Aramean army. The servant was shaking in his sandals and freaking out. Cool headed Elisha takes a look and says "There are more with us than without us!", then, he prays that the eyes of his servant would be open to the spirit realm. Then, he looked and saw horses and chariots of fire surrounding the army. Oh, that we would pray for our eyes to be opened when we feel surrounded.

"For if we died with Him, we shall also live with Him. If we endure, we shall also reign with Him" ...II Timothy 2:11-12. Jesus never promised us that this life would be easy, but, what He does promise is that He will give us the strength to endure until the end. What an awesome beginning to this life's ending; to reign with Christ forever. Don't quit!

How Long?

Lord, how long until Your face shall I see,
How long until Your arms embrace me?
Lord how long until we walk the streets of gold,
Surrounded by the saints, my loved ones I shall hold?
Lord, I know You're still working on me,
And soon I'll hear my name, then together forever we'll be.

By David K. McClain

Sometimes, God will take you down paths that you don't understand in order to get you where He wants you to be. If you are currently on that path, stay focused and don't lose sight of the path, your destination may not be His.

Colossians 2:2 ..."to the knowledge of the mystery of God, both of the Father and of Christ, in whom are hidden all the treasures of wisdom and knowledge." "Knowledge and faith make a soul rich. The stronger our faith, and the warmer our love, the more will our comfort be. The treasures of wisdom are hid, not from us, but for us, in Christ." (Matthew Henry)

"Where can I go from Your spirit? Or where can I flee from Your presence? If I ascend into heaven, You are there; if I make my bed in hell, behold, You are there." Psalm 139:7, 8 ...in other words, you can run, but you cannot hide!

The sword crafted by the hands of man, or, the living word of God? Which will you take into your battles? Hebrews 4:12 ..."For the word of God is living and powerful, and sharper than any two edged sword, piercing even to the division of soul and spirit, and of joints and marrow, and is a discerner of the thoughts and intents of the heart." NKJV

Luke 9:13, 14 ..."When the disciples expressed concern about where the crowd of thousands would eat, Jesus offered a surprising solution: "You feed them." The disciples had focused their attention on what they didn't have--food and money. Do you think that God would ask you to do something that together you and He couldn't handle?" (Tindale).

"Bring me joy bring me peace, bring the chance to be free, bring me anything that brings You glory. And I know there'll be days when this life brings me pain, but if that's what it takes to praise You, Jesus, bring the rain"... (Mercy Me; Bring the Rain)

Whenever it gets dark, we turn on a light. God's word works the same way in that whenever we need direction, we should turn to the Bible for guidance. That way, we are investing in the long term Christ centered solutions where we want to be "established". Psalm 119:133 "Direct" (establish) "my footsteps in thy Word..."

When God calls me home... this is what I envision happening. Makes me want to go today!

Michael English Video – "I Bowed on My Knees"

And now, for something deep: Fuzzy saw a bear, the bear saw Fuzzy, the bear was bulgy, the bulge was Fuzzy. I am sure there is a moral somewhere in this story, I just haven't been able to find it yet.

The word of God spreads like ripples on a pond where, from a single center, each wave touches the next, spreading wider and farther. Just be part of the wave touching those around you, who in turn will touch others until all is felt by the movement of the Word. Never feel that your part is unimportant or insignificant.

When the storms of life seem to surround you, and the sea's waves seem higher than you can handle. When the burdens you carry seem so heavy that you are sinking. When it seems like there's no way out... THERE IS! There is One who is right beside you. There is One who calms the sea's and hushes the storms. His name is Jesus! "Cast your burdens upon the Lord, and He shall sustain you,..." Psalm 55:22

What possibly can this world offer you? Possessions will disappoint you. Governments will disappoint you. Relationships will disappoint you. NOTHING that this world can offer will bring you eternal peace. ONLY Jesus can satisfy your searching soul. "Do not lay up for yourselves treasures on earth, but lay up for yourselves treasures in heaven. For where your treasure is, there will your heart be also." Matthew 6:19-21

Since happiness is based on circumstances, are your circumstances making you happy? Seek the Lord and you will find happiness through Him, not circumstances! Psalm 28:7

As long as man seeks what is right in his own eyes, his vision will be blurred! "Seek first the kingdom of God and His righteousness and all these things will be added unto you." Matthew 6:33

When we look at our problems, they seem too big to conquer. When God looks at our problems, they are already conquered. Let go and let God! "These things I have spoken to you, that in me you may have peace. In the world you will have tribulation; but, be of good cheer, I have overcome the world."... Jesus

What problem have you ever solved by worrying about it? A worried mind is a troubled mind that is not at peace. We worry because we lack knowledge of the future. Worry replaced by prayer equals trust.

Instead of worrying about something you have no control of, why not pray and trust God who has ALL control? 1 Peter 5:7

Now, a quick lesson from the book of Jeremiah. QUESTION: Does life start at conception or at birth? ANSWER: Neither!! Jeremiah 1:5 "BEFORE I formed you in the womb I knew you; BEFORE you were born I sanctified you; I ordained you a prophet to the nations." Long before you were a "spark" in your parents eye... God knew you! You were created by God to bring glory to God... therefore... BRING IT!!

A good reminder for us!

Casting Crowns – "Praise You In The Storm" YouTube.Com

What If?

What if God hadn't sent His son
as Savior of this earth,
There'd be no star, no manger scene,
there'd be no virgin birth.
BUT, God loves this world so much,
He DID send His own son.
His reason was to give the gift
of salvation to everyone.
So, as this season brings you gifts,
and presents that you love,
Let's not forget the greatest gift,
sent from God above.

By David K. McClain

Revelation 6:12 ..."and the moon became as blood."

Total Lunar Eclipse - December 21, 2010

Psalm 121:2 "My help comes from the Lord."

Dead people don't have problems! ROMANS 6:10, 11 "For the death that He died, He died to sin once for all; but the life that He lives, He lives to God. Even so, consider yourselves to be DEAD to sin, but ALIVE to God in Christ Jesus." Dying to self is the only way to live... To be TOTALLY dependent upon Jesus Christ is where life and the answer to your problems and sorrows begin.

January 13 MSN headline: Wobbly earth means your horoscope is wrong. Stars shifted over 2000 years so horoscope signs are nearly a month off. ISAIAH 40:26 "Lift up your eyes on high, and see who has created these things" (stars) ...Instead of looking to the horoscope and stars trying to figure your future, look to the ONE who created the stars and KNOWS your future.

"The love of God is greater far than tongue or pen can ever tell; it goes beyond the highest star, and reaches to the lowest hell; the guilty pair, bowed down with care, God gave His Son to win; His erring child He reconciled, and pardoned from his sin." (Fredrick Martin Lehman 1917)

Yep... Summer is almost here, I can see the deer walking in the back yard!

"All that is necessary for the triumph of evil is that good men do nothing!"
(Edmund Burke 1784)

"A lie will travel half way around the world before the truth can get its pants on." (Winston Churchill)

Thank You

There was one point in time when each one of you crossed my life's path with yours. I consider myself to be the most fortunate man alive. "Things" will come and go in our lives, only relationships and true friendships will last a lifetime. I thank the good Lord for each of you and the blessings you have brought to my life. Thank you for your prayers. I made it to the half century mark... I LOVE YOU!

No Fear

Dictionary definition of FEAR- A painful emotion or passion excited by the expectation of evil... Hmmm... so fear is expecting something bad to happen before it even happens. Now, Gods solution to fear... 2 Timothy 1:7 "For God did not give us a spirit of fear, but of power and love and sound mind." Sound mind... How does one get a sound mind? Romans 1...

Christ is bigger than the crisis!

Not Carnality But Christ

"Put temporal things in your life to make you happy and you will be happy temporarily. Put eternal things in your life to make you complete and you will be complete for eternity. --If then you were raised in with Christ, seek those things which are above, where Christ is, sitting at the right hand of God. Set your affections (mind) on the things above, not on the things of the earth. For you died, and your life is hidden with Christ in God. When Christ who is our life appears, then you also will appear with Him in glory."-- Colossians 3:1-4

Thank you ALS Association for providing the handicap van so I could celebrate Easter Sunday with my family.

Death is not a period, it is just a comma. For those born again, to be absent from the body is to be present with the Lord.

Now or Then?

In the game of chess, you have the royalty of the King and Queen, the wisdom and knowledge of the Bishop, the craftiness and skills of the Knight, the cleverness of the Rook and the selflessness of the Pawn. However, when the game is over, all of the pieces are put into a box or tucked away into a drawer and their titles, skills and abilities mean nothing. There is coming a day when the "game" of this life will end for each of us. All of our titles, skills and abilities will mean nothing. All that will matter is what we decided to do with the saving knowledge of Jesus Christ. Did you accept Him as Lord of your life or did you reject Him? Will the first words you hear Jesus say to you be "Well done my good and faithful servant, enter in." or will you hear Him say "Depart from me, I never knew you!"? Either you will confess Him as Lord of your life now, while there is still time, or, you will confess Him as Lord then, when it is too late. Philippians 2:9-11 "Therefore, God has highly exalted Him and given Him the name which is above every name, that at the name of Jesus every knee shall bow, of those in heaven, and of those on earth, and of those under the earth, and that every tongue shall confess that Jesus Christ is Lord, to the glory of God the Father."

Know how to get out of trouble before it comes... Psalm 34:19 "Many are the afflictions of the righteous, but the Lord delivers him out of them ALL." DONT PANIC!

"In every difficulty there is an opportunity. In order to see that opportunity, you must look for it. That means looking clearly and objectivity at the problem, laying out a plan of attack, then, getting after it. What You Refuse To Overcome, Will Eventually Overcome You..."
(New Life Devotions)

Strong Christians aren't strong people, they just know where to run.

Jesus took your curse of death so you can take His blessing of life.

To be alone with God is to be in the majority.

God gave you the world, get out of your closet and enjoy the gifts of God. ENJOY LIFE!

"Character is what you are in the dark." (D.L. Moody)

Learn to trouble your troubles rather than allowing your troubles to trouble you!

You cannot have a testimony without a test!

Be Yoked To Jesus Or Be Choked By The World!!

A YOKE is a wooden beam, normally used between a pair of oxen or other animals to enable them to pull a load together while working in the field. The yoke is designed to distribute the weight of the load evenly. Though the yoked animals have many duties such as dragging logs or boulders, pulling a cart or turning a grinding wheel, the most common use is pulling a plow in the fields to prepare for the planting of crops. The two animals have to be of the same breed and strength. If you were to match an ox with a donkey, chances are that the rows of plowed soil would look more like circles than straight lines. You cannot have two animals unequally yoked and expect harmony at the plow. In the book of Mathew chapter 11, verses 28-30, Jesus says "Come unto me, ALL who are weary and heavy laden, and I will give you rest. Take my YOKE upon you and learn from me, for I am gentle and humble in heart; and you will find rest in your soul. For MY yoke is easy and MY load is light." When a young ox is being trained, it will often times be paired up with an older, more mature ox. The older ox will carry the load until the young ox gains its strength and can pull its share of the load. Jesus gives us a mental picture of the yoke so we can associate it with His message that we don't have to carry life's burden alone. Why is it that when the weight of the world feels like it's on our shoulders that we often look to the world for the answers?? This world can offer us NOTHING!! Let's not forget who the "god" of this world is as he seeks to devour those who are vulnerable. The book of 2 Corinthians 4:4 says: "In their case the god of this world (Satan) has blinded the eyes of the unbeliever, to keep them from seeing the light of the gospel of the glory of Christ, who is the image of God." Sadly, the enemy has blinded the believer as well from seeking the yoke of Christ to carry their burdens. You cannot be yoked to this world and expect peace, joy and harmony in your spirit, just ain't gonna happen. Jesus simply tells us to "YOKE" to Him and HE will carry the load. Remember, greater is HE (Jesus) who is in us (the believer) than he (Satan) who is in the world! Be YOKED with Jesus or be CHOKED by the world!!!

You cannot "tell" folks, you have to "show" folks!

The TRUTH!! If you can't hack it, get your jacket!!!

The very nature of God is love. Have you told someone that you love them today?

Armor Up And Get Your Stomp On!

Why is it that at times, the Christian walk of faith seems more like a crawl for survival? How is it that at times, we allow the enemy to convince us that we are defeated? God has given to each of us ALL of the weapons that we need to stand up and confront the enemy face to face. It's time that we draw a line in the sand and say "ENOUGH IS ENOUGH!!!" In the book of Ephesians 6:13-18, God gives us the key to stand with confidence and fight with victory. -- "Therefore take up the whole armor of God that you may be able to withstand in the evil day, and having done all, to stand. Stand therefore, having girded your waist with truth, having put on the breastplate of righteousness, having shod your feet with the preparation of the gospel of peace; ABOVE ALL, taking the shield of faith with which you will be able to quench ALL of the fiery darts of the wicked one. And take the helmet of salvation, and the sword of the Spirit, which is the word of God; praying always with all prayer and supplication in the Spirit, being watchful to this end with all perseverance and supplication for all the saints."-NKJV-- Now, I have read this many many, many times and NO WHERE does it mention a back plate... retreat IS NOT an option from God! God gave us this armor not as a fashion statement, but as our weapon to "take it to the devil!" We must remember, the battle has already been won! Satan was defeated when Christ arose from the grave. "ALL authority was given to Jesus and He has anointed us (those born again-John 3:3) with the power to stand against the principalities, against powers, against the rulers of the darkness of this age and against spiritual hosts of wickedness in the heavenly places." Satan is a liar and deceiver, He has absolutely NO authority or power over you, the only "say so" he has on you is only what you allow him over you. Stop listening to lies and start doing some STOMPING! If you have something to say to the devil, write it on the bottom of your shoe!!! The next time the devil comes knocking, simply ask Jesus to answer. Armor up and get your stomp on!! (DKM)

"Has fear ever solved a problem or crisis? Hope has! Faith has! JESUS has!!"
(Max Lucado)

Above all else, guard your heart, for everything you do flows from it.

Romans 12:2--"To transform your mind is to think about where you're going, not where you've been" (T.D. Jakes)

TEMPORARILY Disabled... 1 Peter 1:6-9

"Jesus, friend of sinners, break our hearts with what breaks yours!" (Casting Crowns).

Another article with a little more detail:
Breakthrough could lead to effective treatment for ALS | The Republic
Chicago — Researchers say they found a common cause behind the mysterious and deadly affliction of amyotrophic lateral sclerosis, better known as Lou Gehrig's disease that could lead to an effective treatment.
THEREPUBLIC.COM

The Lord will show you the door, but, you have to reach for the knob.

A word to those being tempted: ...When the fire is in the fireplace, there is warmth, there is light, comfort and contentment. BUT, pull the fire out of the hearth and risk danger, pain and the possibility of losing everything! KEEP THE FIRE WHERE IT BELONGS!!!

YAWN: An honest opinion openly expressed!

The odds of being eaten by a shark are 300 million to 1. The odds of dying from a dog bite is 20 million to 1. The odds of being struck by lightning this year are 700,000 to 1. The odds of dying from falling in your bathtub are 685,000 to 1. The odds of being hit by this 6 ton space station that will crash to the earth this weekend are 3,000 to 1. I HIGHLY recommend that you wear a helmet this weekend!

There is sun behind the dark clouds, the clouds are only temporary.

"Why can't anything EVER go my way?" Ever thought that before? Maybe you are thinking this now. Isaiah 55:8 "For My thoughts are not your thoughts, neither your ways My ways, says the Lord." What you perceive as "Not going your way" may very well be exactly where God wants you. Turn your trial into triumph by trusting God to lead you through it.

Lord, help me to bloom where I am planted!

What do you do when you don't know what to do?.... TRUST! Proverbs 3:5-6 "Trust in the Lord with all of your heart and lean not on your own understanding, acknowledge the Lord in all of your ways, and He will direct your path."

The mystery has been solved!!! Colossians 1:26-27 "...the MYSTERY which has been hidden from ages and from generations, but now has been revealed to His Saints. To them God willed to make known what are the riches of the glory of this mystery"... which is... (drum roll)... "CHRIST IN YOU!!!" Is He?

THE WORD of GOD! The most powerful weapon on earth!!!

Look Inside
You're My King!
Lord, lead me to the Rock, that is higher than I,
Lest I should stumble, lest I should die.
Set me on your cliff, to where I cannot hide,
Exposing my heart, Lord, please look inside.

By David K. McClain

"In the beginning was the Word (Jesus), and the Word was with God, and the Word was God. He (Jesus) was in the beginning with God. All things were made through Him, and without Him nothing was made that was made. In Him was life, and the life was the light of men. And the light shines in the darkness, and the darkness did not comprehend it." John 1:1-5. Got God? Get God and get life, get life and become the light.... John 3:16

"Be faithful unto death and I will give you the Crown Of Life!" (Jesus)

"Therefore we do not lose heart. Even though our outward man is perishing, yet the inward man is being renewed day by day. For our light infliction, which is but for a moment, is working for us a far more exceeding and eternal weight of glory, while we do not look at the things that are seen, but at the things that are not seen. For the things that are seen are temporary, but the things that are not seen are eternal." 2 Cor. 4:16-18 Stop focusing on the temporary clouds that come and go in your life, rather, focus on the SON who evaporates the clouds.

Thank the Lord for generators! 8 inches of snow and no power, that is, until Josh turned on the generator... ahhhh... breathing again!

"That your faith should not stand in the wisdom of men, but in the power of God"... 1Cor.2:5. If you try to base saving faith on the "wisdom of men", it ceases to be saving faith.

Romo time!

28-0

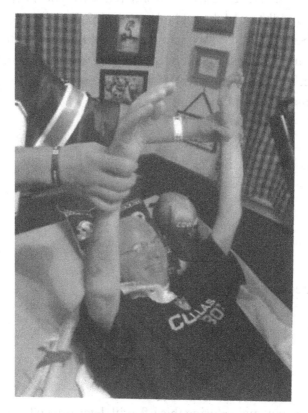

Ben McClain with David Kurt McClain

Just because situations change, doesn't mean they have to change you!

"Walk in the Spirit, and you will not fulfill the lust of the flesh. For the flesh lusts against the Spirit, and the Spirit against the flesh; and these are contrary to one another, so you do not do the things that you wish"... Galatians 5:16-17. We all have a dog fight within ourselves, our flesh against the Spirit, the dog that wins will be the dog you feed the most.

Just a thought: Have you ever wondered why you never hear the names of Buddha or Mohamad taken in vain? These names are of no threat to Satan. "JESUS; the name above all names. At the mention of His name, demons are silenced, the sick are healed and the lost are found. At the mention of His name, every knee will bow..." Philippians 2:10 Just a thought!

Christmas Day forecast... SON!

Thank you Lord for another year! 12-31

Jesus is the Reason for ALL seasons!!

It is a great day to be alive... encourage someone today.

The decision you make during this life will determine where you spend your next... "For God so loved the world (YOU), that He gave His only son, that whosoever (YOU) will believe in Him, will not perish but have everlasting life"... just saying because God said it! John 3:16

Sometimes our KNOW just needs to know!

Psalm 46:10 "Be still and KNOW that I am God..."

Okay... check it out... "Blessed is the King who comes in the name of the Lord!" "Peace in heaven and Glory in the highest!" Some of the Pharisee's in the crowd said to Jesus, "Teacher, rebuke your disciples!" "I tell you," he replied, "If they keep quiet, the stones will cry out!!"... What'll you say that we give the stones the day off?!... Luke 19:38-40

What one does with his or her life far outweighs the number of years he or she will live. Its quality, not quantity. You have nothing to do with the number of days God will give you, however, you have everything to do with the testimony He gives you and how you present yourself to others. Live to love!

Rewards To Come

Try not to dwell on your current heartache, pain, sickness or suffering ... rather ...focus on the rewards yet to come....

"...Therefore we do not lose heart. Even though our outward man is perishing, yet the inward man is being renewed day by day. For our light affliction, which is with us for but a moment, is working for us a far more exceeding and eternal weight of glory, while we do not look at the things that are seen, but at the things that are not seen. For the things that are seen are temporary, but the things that are not seen are eternal." 2 Corinthians 4

What I hang my hat on.

If you are feeling far away from. God... WHO MOVED???

Think about it before you say it... once it leaves your lips, it cannot be retrieved.

Stop seeing yourself through the eyes of others and start seeing yourself through the eyes of God.

"It is better to try something big and fail than to do nothing and succeed!" (Unknown)

"There is no drug or alcohol high that can come close to the high from serving and living for Jesus Christ." (Johnny Cash)

Looking for peace of mind? Look no further!
"He is at perfect peace whose mind is steadfast on You"
Isaiah 26:3

While there is life ...there is hope!!

Psalm 71:5 "For You are my hope, OH LORD GOD..."

Are you in your hour of pain and sorrow? Hang on, stay strong, joy is on the way!

John 16:16-17 "A woman, when she is in labor, has sorrow because her hour is come; but as soon as she has given birth to the child, she no longer remembers the anguish, for a human being has been born into the world."... "Therefore you now have sorrow; but I will see you again and your heart will rejoice, and your joy no one will take from you."

Is your life feeling empty and dark? Step into the Light and be filled forever! John 12:46 "I have come as a light into the world, that whoever believes in me should not abide in darkness."

Gods first act of creation was to separate light from darkness, He's been doing the same ever since.

3/4/12

David Kurt McClain shared a page
March 9, 2012

The David and Donna McClain 'Fifty for 50' House
Non-Profit Organization
Part of the "Building Team" (in blue) in Dominican Republic
Jacob Mazeika (nephew) Kathleen & Ben with recipient of new house

Things That Matter

After a hundred years, will that new car really matter? Will the square footage in your home be worth anything? Can you take that promotion into eternity? Don't let the things of this world cloud your vision for heaven.

IF you don't give up, you CANNOT be defeated!!

When a circus trapeze artist knows that he has a net under him, he becomes one without fear. The net provides confidence, security and safety to his endeavors. So is true with our walk with the Lord, we can be confident and secure through Him. God is not only our Righteousness, He is our RighteousNET... NO FEAR!!

Let us be like sheep who know the Shepherd.

"Mind over matter... if you don't mind, it doesn't matter!!" (John Hagee)

Sometimes, God will take you down paths that you don't understand in order to get you where He wants you to be. If you are currently on that path, stay focused and don't lose sight of the path, your destination may not be His.

I don't focus on what I can't do, I focus on what God can do through me.

Statistics told me that I had 1 to 3 years to live once I was diagnosed with ALS. I am now on my 10th year. I thank the Good Lord that I live by the grace of God and not by statistics. 2012

Tired of looking to the world to bring you that inner peace only to be disappointed ...over and over again? Stop living WITHOUT and start looking WITHIN!!!.... John 14:27 "Peace I leave with you, My peace I give to you: NOT as the world gives do I give to you. Let not your heart be troubled, neither let it be afraid."

When you are physically at the well... you WILL get a drink!!! John 7:38 "Whosoever believes in me, as scripture has said, rivers of living water will flow from within them."

"Not even the angels can separate you from the love of God." Romans 8.38 and 39... check it out!

Live like there's nothing to fear ....there isn't!!! 2 Timothy 1.7

Dwell ON the Word and the Word will dwell WITHIN you!!!

John chapter 1 ..."In the beginning was the Word, and the Word was with God, and the Word was God..... But as many as received Him, to them He gave the right to become the children of God, to those who believe in His name..... And the Word became flesh and dwelt among us, and we beheld His glory..."

Stepping out on the town tomorrow night... well ...maybe not "stepping" ...more like wheelchairing. Anyway, gonna go see Anthony Evans (contestant on last season's "The Voice") who will be doing a benefit concert for Turning Point Rehabilitation Center.

Okay, there's a mosquito on my forehead and I can't move... hate when that happens!

Every day is Father's Day to me, I have the greatest kids! The best Father's Day gift will be the day I hold my wife once again and hug my kids. I will NOT give up until that day happens!

If you're wondering why Dad's not responding, his eye-scan machine is having mechanical problems. My mom will be calling technical support tomorrow, so hopefully they can get it fixed soon! –Kathleen

Finally got a computer eye scan that works. Ahhh... I can talk again ... or... shall I say... I can blink again!

Come you sinners lost and lonely, Jesus blood can set you free, for He saved the worst among you, when He saved a wretch like me. (Yes, I know... GVB)

I was just told by my friend Becky that while on a hike, she saw me in eagle form... bald!! LOL

It's not about what I think, It's about what God says.

"Well I've had the chance to gain the world and live just like a King, but, without Your (Jesus) love it doesn't mean a thing!..." (Keith Green-I Pledge My Head To Heaven)

Going out on the town with my family tonight... Christian concert... gonna be fun!

Ben McClain with David Kurt McClain and Ashley, Josh, Donna, and Anthony Evans Jr.
November 28, 2012 Instagram

"We got to go backstage and meet Anthony Evans Jr.! It's great to see someone in his position be so humble! We gave him my dad's letter too!" Ben McClain

Your life's journey is a process, try to enjoy every step of the way.

For You are my HOPE, Oh Lord God!

Quotes About Anything and Everything

February 25, 2013

A psychologist walked around a room while teaching stress management to an audience. As she raised a glass of water, everyone expected they'd be asked the "half empty or half full" question. Instead, with a smile on her face, she inquired: "How heavy is this glass of water?" Answers called out ranged from 8 oz. to 20 oz.

She replied, "The absolute weight doesn't matter. It depends on how long I hold it. If I hold it for a minute, it's not a problem. If I hold it for an hour, I'll have an ache in my arm. If I hold it for a day, my arm will feel numb and paralyzed. In each case, the weight of the glass doesn't change, but the longer I hold it, the heavier it becomes." She continued, "The stresses and worries in life are like that glass of water. Think about them for a while and nothing happens. Think about them a bit longer and they begin to hurt. And if you think about them all day long, you will feel paralyzed – incapable of doing anything."

It's important to remember to let go of your stresses. As early in the evening as you can, put all your burdens down. Don't carry them through the evening and into the night. Remember to put the glass down!

Find something every day to be thankful for. If it is a person ...tell them!

Has your light gone dim, or worse yet, gone out?

Seasons of Our Life:
Part Three

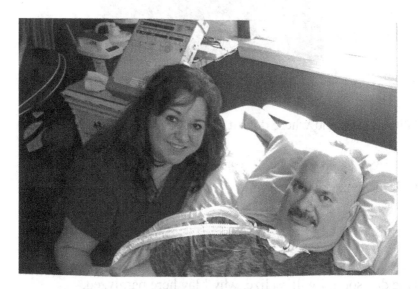

Donna & David
After 30 years of marriage

David K. McClain 11-17-13

What is dust and where does it come from??

In Jesus name ...we press on.

One Day Soon

One day soon, I will realize, why I lay here paralyzed.
One day soon, I will realize, why I have to speak with my eyes.
One day soon, my idle tongue, will sing all praises to the SON.
One day soon, my lungs so weak, will provide the air for me to speak.
One day soon, my arms so still, will hug and hold those who will.
One day soon, my legs so frail, will jump and dance, a miracle unveiled.
One day soon, I will hear Him call, then I will realize ...IT WAS WORTH IT ALL.

By David K. McClain
11-22-13

I was staring out the window the other day and started imagining what I can't imagine so I jotted down

I Can't Imagine What to Imagine

I cant imagine what to imagine, I cant see what's to be seen,
My eyes are temporarily blinded of the sights that soon I'll see.
When my eyes are finally opened, in glory I will be,
I will see the Lamb of God, who gave His life for me.
My eyes will then behold Him, I'll bow and call Him King,
I'll join with all of heaven, a new song to Him I'll sing.

I cant imagine what to imagine,
I can't hear the sounds to be heard,
My ears are not yet opened, but soon I'll hear His words,
"Well done my faithful servant" are the words I hold so dear,
"Enter into my kingdom", from His lips I want to hear.
Sounds of praise and adoration, forever and ever will be,
As all of heaven will sing, in perfect harmony.

I can't imagine what to imagine, looking through a prism clear,
As colors of the rainbow suddenly appear. Colors not yet known, never seen before,
Will soon be revealed, at the foot of heavens door.
No sun, no moon, no stars, and yet a brilliant light,
Shining from His glory, such a magnificent sight.
Darkness gone forever, cold, damp days are done,
We'll be warmed in His very presence, the presence of the SON.

I can't imagine what to imagine, when time shall be no more,
No hours no days no years to count, no centuries as before.
No appointments to keep, no reasons to rush, pressure no more there'll be,
Just worship and praise where we'll be amazed, for all of eternity.

97

I can't imagine what to imagine, when the need to imagine will cease,
I'll be in the reality of the Promised Land, living in perfect peace.

Song written by David K. McClain
8-26-10

eternal peace.

Love knows no boundaries

Hello everybody- this is Jeff. David was brought to the ER last night for what we think is a kidney stone again. We just got admitted into a room about an hour ago. Thankfully, he said that the pain has gone away, meaning he may have passed it or it may have shifted. His white blood cell count was also high last night so the docs are looking to see if there's an infection or if it was caused by the stone and the pain. All things considered, he's doing well but tired. Please pray for wisdom for the docs, that The Lord would show them what to do, or show them that He's already done it so that David could go home soon. He's a champ! Please also pray for Donna and the family for wisdom and rest. Thank you!

Update- thank you all for praying, please keep them coming! David does have a pretty big stone (6.5 mm) but is doing well today. The Lord has thankfully shifted the stone a bit so that it is not causing him any pain. The plan is to put in a stent in the morning, then check to make sure there is no infection behind the blockage. If it is clear the doc will break up the stone with a laser and remove it. If there is infection he will have to take antibiotics until it is cleared up before breaking up the stone which could take a while. Please pray that there is no infection. On behalf of David and the family, thank you again for the prayers and encouraging words! Much love to you all!

UPDATE: Praise the Lord, Dad's procedure went very well! There was no infection and the doctor was able to remove the stone. Lord willing, he will be heading back home around 4pm. The stent will be removed next Wednesday. Thank you all do much for your prayers, it's clear that Dad has been strengthened by them! -Kat and Jeff

David Kurt McClain

YeeeeeeeeeeHaaaaaaaaaaaaaw!!!... I am home. They removed the golf ball from my ureter... whew!!!! THANK YOUR PRAYERS... they worked.
I am whooped... chat with you tomorrow.

Don't start out... FINISH out.

Believe RIGHT and you will live RIGHT

HELP.... somehow, I changed the language to Japanese, I was sick the day that they taught Japanese in school. All I see are symbols. Can anybody help this Japanese illiterate Texan out?

12/31/13

Happy New Year

"To your dreams stay big, and your worries stay small, I hope you know somebody loves you..."

"My Wish" by Rascal Flatts

Will this be the year?

The battle belongs to the Lord.

After the shadows, there will be sunshine.

Have you baited your hook lately? Matthew 4:19-20 ...Then He said to them "Follow Me, and I will make you fishers of men. They immediately left their nets and followed Him."

From one scarred hand to another.

Take charge of your life ...or ...somebody else will.

I want to take a moment to thank each and every one of you who wished me a happy birthday. It was an awesome day. Since becoming ill, my priorities have completely changed. I no longer look to material things to make me happy or to bring me joy. My joy and happiness comes from the relationships that I have with my Lord and Savior Jesus Christ, my family and ...YOU ...my many friends. Material things are temporary and will come and go, but, relationships last an eternity. Thank you again and know that you are loved by me.

So, I am not able to use legs to walk with you, I am not able to use my arms to give you a hug, I am not able to use my voice to tell you that I love you, but, I CAN smile... so... I will walk with you, give you a hug and tell you that I love you all with just my smile.

This is Ben on my dad's page. His eye-scan computer broke so we are waiting for them to fix it or give us a loaner. Please pray that either one happens soon! Until then, back to the eye chart for communicating! "Would you like to buy a vowel, dad?"

Thank you Ann and Mark Giangarra for fixing my computer.

God... what do You want me to do today??

Lord, I believe, help now my unbelief.

Get Up and Try Again

When this life seems SO hard and you just can't win,
when you are down for the count and you've lost your wind,
when the ice is so thin that you keep falling in,
GET UP and try again.
...where there's a will, there's a way.

When they say to your face that it can't be done,
but, you know in your heart that they are wrong,
just dig deep, stay on your feet, and keep moving on,
so GET UP and try again.
...where there is no vision, the people will perish.

When the mountains so steep that you just can't climb.
And the path is so rough that you feel like crying,
just call on the Lord and His strength you will find,
so, GET UP and try again.
...mountain be moved.

When you try so hard, day after day,
and the fruits of your labor don't seem to stay,
your dreams, goals and visions may be one "GET UP" away,
so, GET UP and try again..
...don't quit!

By David K. McClain
4-10-2014

You become what you feed your mind... Romans 12:1, 2

God does not debate His existence........ He declares it

God is omnipotent, omnipresent and omniscient.

Omnipotent means that God is all-powerful. He spoke all things into being, and all things -- every cell, every breath, every thought -- are sustained by Him. There is nothing too difficult for Him to do.
-- Jeremiah 32:17, 18, 26, 27 --

Omnipresent means that God is everywhere, around everything and close to everyone. "Do not I fill heaven and earth? Declares the Lord."
-- Psalm 139:7-12 --

Omniscient means that God is all-knowing. God's knowledge encompasses every possible thing that exists, has ever existed, or, will ever exist. Nothing is a mystery to God.
-- Psalm 139:1-6 --

God already has your life mapped out, don't be afraid to ask Him to fill you in ...He would love to hear from you.

Let us all learn from the ant, it will NEVER quit and NEVER looks behind.

Faith sees the invisible.

Focus on the opportunity ...not the problem. Many times, you see it as a problem when God will see it as an opportunity.

Our connection to Adam guarantees death. Our connection to Jesus Christ guarantees eternal life.

The only "man-made" things that will be in heaven ...will be ...the holes in HIS hands and feet.

God loves you... God can restore you... God has a purpose for your life.

Fill your heart and mind with God's Words or Satan will fill them with his.

Though God is infinitely far above our ability to fully understand, He tells us through His Word very specific truth's about Himself so that we can know what He is like, and be drawn to worship Him.

God is Jehovah. The name of the independent, self-complete being--"I AM WHO I AM"--only belongs to Jehovah God. His name is forever. Our proper response to Him should be to fall down in fear (reverence of God) and awe of the One who possesses all authority. --Exodus 3:13-15

For those who are born again (John 3:1-7, 16), we are set apart.

Sanctify: to set apart, separate, to purify. God is Jehovah (Lord) M'Kaddesh. This name means "the God who sanctifies". Sanctification is the separation of a person to the dedication of the Holy. When the two words are combined -Jehovah and M'Kaddesh- it is translated as "The Lord who sets you apart". --Exodus 31:13; Leviticus 20:8

Holiness of God

"OMG"-are those words of praise and worship, or, are those words of vain repetition? Also, God's last name IS NOT "dammit".

Exodus 20:7 You shall not take the name of the Lord your God in vain.

God's name is Holy.

Holy: Divine power, sacred, worthy of praise and worship, deity, endowed with extreme purity, perfect.

I like how R. C. Sproul explains it: "The holiness of God is the most difficult of God's attributes to explain, partly because it is one of His essential attributes that is not shared, inherently, by man. We only become holy through our relationship in Jesus Christ. It is an imputed holiness." R. C. Sproul

I would rather be strong in ONE (Jesus), than to be weak in many (worldly pleasures).

Do more than nothing.

David McClain's ALS Ice Bucket Challenge!
291,772 views

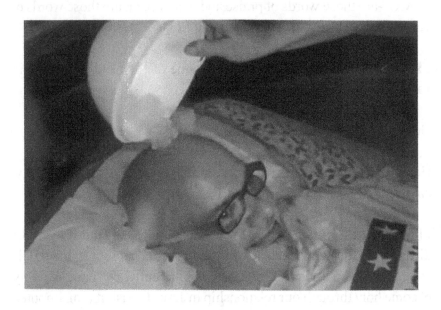

"With the craze of the ALS Ice Bucket Challenge, many people are pouring buckets of water over their heads. There is one local man who is different than the rest! My father-in-law, David Kurt McClain, resides right here in New Haven and currently has ALS...." Ashley McClain 8-19-14

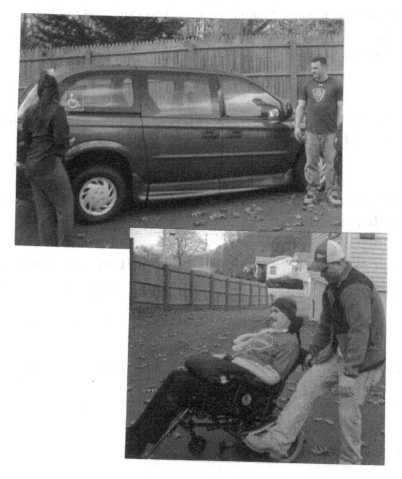

David admiring his van with sons and Ashley

I want to thank each and every one of you who donated to the go fund me, get Tex moving account. Well, you did it. You raised enough money for me to purchase a van. Because of you, Tex can now get moving. Instead of my getting out four times a year, now, I will be able to get out four or five times a month. I am going to see it for the first time today. I only wish that each one of you could be here to share this awesome moment with me. Once again, thank you from the bottom of my heart.

I am sensing a white Thanksgiving, if you can't find me tomorrow, I will be in the back making snow angels, or, should I say, snow exclamation points... Lol

Colossians 3:2 "Set your mind on the things above, not on the things of the earth."

What are you doing living UNDER the circumstances?? It is time to rise above them!!!

Isaiah 40:31 NKJV "But those who wait on the Lord shall renew their strength; they shall mount up with wings like eagles, they shall run and not be weary, they shall walk and not faint."

I really don't care what happens to me, I live in the sovereignty of my Lord Jesus Christ.

Never compromise your convictions.

Apple In My Heart

Once I did an experiment, in my kitchen one Summer night, the objects I used were quite simple, just an apple and a light.

I filled the flashlight with batteries, took an apple from the bin, I placed them both on the table and I was ready to begin.

I shined the beam on the apple, exposing it in the light, half of it shined so rich and so bright, the other half shadowed my sight.

As I looked upon the apple and the shadow opposite the light, I couldn't help but think of my heart, that was shadowed dark as night.

The apple represents sin that I had held in my heart, it looked and tasted so good at first, but soon began to rot.

The shadows are the chains that bound me to my sin, I tried and tried to walk away, but soon would sin again.

Sins burden was more than heavy, much more than I could bear, it drug me to the depths of low, depression and despair.

I felt like my life had no meaning, that no longer I could cope, but then I remembered a special book, and in that book was hope.

The book that I found was the Bible, the very spoken words from God, a love letter to me that would set me free, from the life that I once trod.

The apple of sin was so heavy, and the chains from shadows so tight, but soon I was freed forever, because Jesus is the LIGHT.

He shown His light upon me, exposing my sin from within, confessed it I did and the apple He rid, never to be seen again.

So, if in your heart there's an orchard, or maybe an apple or two, receive the LIGHT and do what's right, and He will see you through.

By David Kurt McClain
10-2012

On The Holy Spirit

Is it me, or does anybody else have a problem wrapping your brains around the Trinity; God the Father, God the Son and God the Holy Spirit -- 3 in 1. We have all heard the different analogies comparing the Trinity to that of water or, an egg. Just between you and me, I have a problem with comparing something that was created to the most High, most Sovereign, most Holy Creator.

Water: water, ice and steam
Egg: shell, yoke and egg whites
Armadillo: shell, skin and innards (see what I mean)

I just guess that this is one of those things that I won't fully understand until I see Him face to face.

Just in case you are wondering, here is why I don't sweat what's happening in this world or why I don't freak out about my physical condition... Philippians 3:20-21 "For our citizenship is in heaven, from which we also eagerly wait for the Savior, the Lord Jesus Christ, who will transform our lowly body that it may be conformed to His glorious body..." SWEET! New bod just waiting for me to fill!!!

Preach the gospel at all times, and when necessary, use words. (Unknown)

"To the guy who invented zero, thanks for nothing." (Woody Paige)

When I am asleep and dreaming, I don't have ALS, I am whole and healthy. I am trying to figure out how I can dream 24 hours each day... Lol

Fear is the opposite of faith.

Make sure that your sprinkler waters your own lawn before you water someone else's, Matthew 7:3 NKJV "And why do you look at the speck in your brothers eye, but do not consider the plank in your own eye?"

A Few Words From My Heart

And now, a few words from my heart. Over the past few years, some of you have asked me how I can maintain a positive attitude while living a paralyzed and motionless life. The answer to that question is "I can't" in and of myself. The fact of the matter is, it is only through my personal relationship with my Lord and Savior Jesus Christ that I can keep on keeping on. I draw my strength and joy from the Word of God. He is the reason that I can smile. My mind is not on the "here and now", but rather on the "there and then". And I'm not talking about tomorrow or next week or next year, I am talking about my eternal home in heaven. Only when I take my eyes off of Him and put them on me does my feeling sorry for myself and depression set in.

SOLUTION: Don't take my eyes off the Lord!! In his song "No Compromise" Keith Green sings "How can I see when my eyes are on me"? That is so true, believe me, I know. Don't get me wrong, I do have my share of cloudy days. Behind every dark cloud is the SON. I am learning to look through the dark clouds. We live in a 4 dimensional world, height, width, length, and space time. In His resurrected body, Jesus shows us a different dimension. In the book of John 20:19, it says,... When the doors were locked... Jesus came and stood in their midst and said to them "Peace be with you"... It is unclear if Jesus walked through the doors or walls (Scripture doesn't say), but, all that I know is, He wasn't there and He suddenly appeared. Some Bible scholars believe that there will be up to 12 dimensions in heaven. I can't even wrap my mind around that. Why am I telling you this? I tell you this because when I cross over, either by the rapture or by old age, I will be like Him. 1 John 3:2 NASV... "But we know that when Christ appears, we shall be like Him, for you we shall see Him as He is." Is that not cool or what? I will have all of the dimensions that Jesus has and "Yes" I will be showing up at your mansion around dinner. Are you picking up what I'm laying down? I will be trading in this old rusty, dusty and crusty body of mine for a brand new body that will never rust, dust or crust and comes with an eternal warranty. The Apostle Paul was a Bible scholar of all Bible scholars, he studied the Scriptures for over 15 years before he started his ministry. Paul had a near death experience where he was briefly in heaven (2 Corinthians 12:1-4), he said that there was no words in his vocabulary that could explain the sights and sounds that he saw and heard. If someone like Paul, who wrote much of the New Testament and saw heaven first hand and was speechless, I can't even imagine what is in store when I get there. What I have to look forward to far outweighs what I am going through. That is why I can stay positive.

A Lesson From the Grape:

Sometimes, a grape needs to be squeezed beyond itself in order to become something great; jam, jelly, juice and wine.

Sometimes, God will allow us to be squeezed beyond ourselves in order that we can become something great.

James 1:1-4 "Brethren, count it all joy when you fall into various trials, knowing that the testing of your faith produces patience. But let patience have its perfect work, that you may be perfect and complete, lacking nothing."

10/23/14

So, I am stepping out (or should I say rolling out) on the town tonight, going to watch Ben perform with the Power Team.

Me with the Power Team

10/27/14

My son Josh saved my life last Thursday night while we were at the Power Team show. So, there we were sitting in the front row watching this big dude called "Timber" snapping Louisville Slugger baseball bats across his back. Timber was on his last bat and then it happened, as the bat snapped, the handle part became airborne end over end and was heading straight for my head. As the projectile was homing in on my head, my life was flashing before me, suddenly, I was reliving my childhood memories running through fields of Texas blue bonnets and catching horned toads. I quickly snapped out of my trance and started mentally preparing myself for the hurtin that I was about to receive. As the bat handle spear was about to strike its round target, I began to pray, "Dear God, please don't let the sharp end hit me!" I was going to leave there with either a huge lump on my head, or, I was going to leave there with a bat handle sticking out of my head, either way, it wasn't going to be pretty. Just before impact, out of nowhere, I saw Josh's hand appear and he caught the wooden missile mid-flight. It was as if he snatched a fly out of the air with chopsticks. I don't think he was even looking. Then, Josh leans over and says "I've got your back". For some reason, the theme song from that old TV series "Kung Fu" kept playing in my head. In my silent voice, I gave Josh a wink and said "Well done Grasshopper". The next time, I am going to wear a football helmet and motorcycle goggles.

Like father like son!

David Kurt McClain.

Ben McClain

David Kurt McClain   Ben McClain

We Can Learn From the Eagles.

All of us have our own set of challenges and problems. Some more serious than others. So many times, we look at our problems as if they are huge brick walls that totally surrounding us. Regardless of how high that the walls may seem, there is always a solution. Never run from your problems, they will eventually catch up with you and seem much bigger than before. The PROBLEM SOLVING SOLUTION, first, take a deep breath, next pray for everybody involved (if applicable), and ask God to give you wisdom, and finally, chip away one brick at a time.

It's been said that an eagle will fly into the storm and use the storms currents to lift it above it. No matter what your storm is, let Jesus be the current to lift you above it.

You serve that which you love.

You are greater than your circumstances.

Nothing formed against me shall stand.

Pay it forward in 2015.

Never change who you are because of the opinions of others.

Timothy 3--"But realize this, that in the last days difficult times will come..."

...Indeed, all who desire to live godly in Christ Jesus WILL be persecuted.

We are punished by good when we are wrong,
We are persecuted by evil when we are right.

Matthew 5:11-12 NASB "Blessed are you when people insult and persecute you, and falsely say all kinds of evil against you because of me. Rejoice and be glad, for your reward in heaven is great."

The god of the world, or, the God of the Word? Hmmmm... No brainer!!!

"Character is what you are in the dark".
-- D. L. Moody --

On Angels

I often hear when a saint passes away; "Heaven just got a new angel", or "Another angel just got his/her wings", or "He/she just became an angel". As sincere and promising as that sounds, it is not true. We do not become angels when we die. It is MUCH better than that. The truth is, when we die and go to heaven, we become even greater than the angels. The angels are spiritual beings who were created by God to be His servants, and God has given them great authority and power to do His will. And at the present time, while we are on this earth, the angels are greater than we are, because God has made us "a bit lower than the heavenly beings" (Psalm 8:5). BUT, the Bible also says that we will be higher than the angels-- (Hebrews 1:1-14, this passage is speaking about the Son (Jesus) being higher than the angels) in heaven, we will be like Christ. Because we are "joint-heirs" with Jesus, in heaven, we will be above the angels. The Bible also says "Do you not know that we will judge angels?" (1 Corinthians 6:3) This verse may be talking about fallen angels (demons) who chose to follow Satan, if that is the case, I hope that God will allow me to judge the fallen angels who came up with the bright idea of ALS, if so, I will show NO mercy!!!

Just Keep Climbing

Nobody starts off on top of the mountain, you must start at the bottom and scratch and claw your way up. You can do all things (within His will) through Christ who gives you strength, even if it means mountain climbing. The path will be easy on some days as well as very hard on other days. No matter how tough that the path may seem, don't give up, you will make it. Whether it be a relationship that you are trying to work out, an illness that you are trying to conquer, a certain goal that you are trying to reach, or just plain life that you are trying to figure out. Just keep climbing. You will encounter just about every obstacle that you can imagine along the way, but, just keep climbing. There will be times when the climbing seems so hard that you can't climb another inch and you feel like giving up, just keep climbing. There will be beautiful days as well as very stormy days, on the days when it is storming so bad that you can't see because you are covered in mud and the wind is trying to blow you off the mountain, just keep climbing. There will be days when you enjoy the company of others, and then there will be days when no one is around and you are feeling all alone, you are never alone, just keep climbing. There will be days when you walk in the green, soft pastures that feel so good under your feet, and then, there will be days when the ground is thorny and the rocks are sharp under your feet, but, regardless of the terrain, just keep climbing. There will be days when the mountain seems so steep that you get depressed, just take it one step at a time never losing sight of the top of the mountain, so, just keep climbing. Sometimes God will allow us to go through various trials (James 1) in order to test our faith and increase our endurance making us stronger so that we will rely on Him through future challenges. God will NEVER give us more than we can handle. You can choose to take the journey by yourself, or, you can call on the ONE who made the mountains and designed the path. Proverbs 3:5-6 "Trust in the Lord with all of your heart and lean not on your own understanding, acknowledge the Lord in all of your ways, and He will direct YOUR PATH." JUST KEEP CLIMBING!!!!

ALS doesn't dictate my number of days... God does!!!

I am alive and blessed!!!

I am going to be a Papaw again. Congrats Jeff and Kathleen!!!

Back or Front?

Are you looking at yourself from the back or the front?

Those of you who crochet or do needle point can relate. When you crochet something, the back of what you are working on looks like a train wreck, the different colored strings or yarn are going every which way, there appears to be no rhyme or reason or pattern to your labor. You can't even tell what the picture is. HOWEVER, when you look at the front side, there is something beautiful. The strings or yarn are stitched together perfectly to make a beautiful picture. Through the eyes of the person who is crocheting, there is beauty.

I Am Who I Am Because You Are Who You Are

I am who I am because You are who You are!
You knew me, before I was a thought,
You loved me, with your life I was bought.

I am who I am because You are who You are!
I am a candle and You are the Flame,
My wick is eternal, Your child I became.

I am who I am because You are who You are!
I was dying of hunger and You gave me Bread,
Your bread is salvation because of Your blood that was shed.

I am who I am because You are who You are!
I was unworthy but You showed me Your grace,
The feast at Your table, You've set me a place.

I am who I am because You are who You are!
Jehovah Jireh, the God who provides,
You met my heart's needs, on that day that You died.

I am who I am because You are who You are!
Your name is "Everlasting", El Olam to be exact,
Always looking forward and never looking back.

I am who I am because You are who You are!
I am who I am because You are "I AM",
Savior, Creator, You are the LAMB.

By David K. McClain 1/15

David Kurt McClain

On the lighter side of life:

Lizzy saw her pet bear,

her pet bear saw Lizzy,

the bear was bulgy,

the bulge was Lizzy.

The moral of this story: Choose carefully who you hang around, they just may be a wolf in a bears clothing waiting to devour you.

Father God, what is my mission for today???

God doesn't call the qualified... He qualifies the called.

Stop drop and roll won't work in hell!!

I am crawling through the thorns of this life to reach the green pastures in the next!!

Hope is the last thing to die.

"Now hope does not disappoint, because the love of God has been poured out in our hearts by the Holy Spirit who was given to us" Romans 5:5

Where your mind goes, your body will follow.

"Finally brethren" (and sisterern), "whatsoever things are true, "honest, "just, "pure, "lovely," of good report, if there be any virtue (moral excellence), if there be any praise, THINK on these things."
Philippians 4:8

When you are in it deep and over your head... That's when you know what you are made of.

So, you tried it, and fell flat on your face. It is NEVER too late to try it again... So... GET UP and try it again!!!

Whatever it is.

In one month from today, my granddaughter, SIENNA GRACE, is due to make her grand appearance into this world. She is scheduled to come out and take a look around on March 4th, but, I wouldn't mind if she delayed her entrance until the 7th, which is my birthday. Get on out of there SIENNA GRACE, Papaw is waiting.

"Jesus is the ROCK that rolled my blues away."
-- Larry Norman --

"But I have this treasure in my earthen vessel, so that the surpassing greatness of the power will be of God and not from myself; I am afflicted in every way, but NOT crushed; perplexed, but NOT despairing; persecuted, but NOT forsaken; struck down, but NOT destroyed -- always carrying about in my body the dying

126

of Jesus, so that the life of Jesus also may be manifested in my body."
-- 2 Corinthians 4:7-10 --

Last week, I was chatting to a friend and I asked him how his day was going, his reply was "Okay... Considering." CONSIDERING??? You let "considering" dictate how your day is going to go?
Psalm 118:24 "This is the day that the Lord has made; we will rejoice and be glad in it."

Sometimes you need to be emptied in order to be filled.

You cannot have authority over that which you fear; without help.

-- Matthew 28:18 -- And Jesus came up and spoke to them, saying, "All authority has been given to Me in heaven and on earth."

One of the many many benefits of being born again is; we have the COMPLETE authority over ANY fear through our Lord Jesus Christ.

-- Isaiah 41:10 --"Fear not, for I am with you; be not dismayed (distressed), for I am your God. I will strengthen you, Yes, I will help you, I will uphold you with my righteous right hand."

NO MORE FEAR!!!!!!!!!

Some of you have heard this analogy:
We each have 2 dogs in our life, one is called the flesh and the other is called the Spirit, the one that grows is the one that you feed.

Starve the flesh!!

I love you Lord, and I lift my voice,
to worship You oh my soul, rejoice,
Take joy my King, in what You hear,
May it be a sweet, sweet sound in Your ear.
(Praise chorus)
I have been singing this chorus in my head all morning. There is coming a day when I will stand face to face with my King where I will raise my hands and sing this chorus at the top of my lungs.

Red Hot Jawbreakers

I use to love those red hot jawbreakers called "fire balls", the name does not do them justice. Molten lava balls would be a more appropriate name for them. I will never forget my last experience with one years ago. They were a little smaller than a golf ball and have a reddish, rusty orange color, which should have been a red flag. When I took it out of the wrapper, it was smoking, which should have been a second red flag (just kidding, it wasn't smoking... Yet!!). I popped it in my mouth and it started off tasting very sweet and wimpy. As time went by, the heat really started to crank up and Kick in. Ten minutes into the thing, beads of sweat were forming on my brow. "Ewwwwee, it is getting hot in here, someone needs to open the window!!!" As I was approaching the core of this lethal white hot jawbreaker, I was beginning to realize that this wasn't going to have a happy ending. The core of the jawbreaker is where they hide the mixture of habanero peppers, jalapeno peppers and nitro glycerin. By now, I was in full sweat mode, my taste buds were fusing together and I had a 5 alarm fire going on in my mouth. I was thinking burn center at the hospital but I had to wait for the feeling to return to my face. Why didn't I choose a watermelon flavored jolly rancher instead??

In a way, sin is a lot like eating a fire ball jawbreaker. Sin will ALWAYS starts tasting sweet, looking beautiful, feeling good and having fun, however, the longer that you live in sin the closer you are to getting burned and it will ultimately destroy you.

Face to face with sin, you better think again!!

1 John 1:9 "If we confess our sins, He is faithful and just to forgive us our sins and cleanse us from all unrighteousness."

Know Who Your Enemy Is!!

-- 2 Corinthians 10:3-5 "For though we walk in the flesh, we do not war according to the flesh. For the weapons of our warfare are not carnal but are mighty in God for pulling down strongholds, casting down imaginations and every high thing that exalts itself against the knowledge of God, bringing EVERY thought into captivity to the obedience to Christ."

"Casting down Imaginations... Bringing EVERY thought into captivity..."

Our mind is the engine that drives our bodies. The enemy (Satan) knows this and is constantly trying to control our mind through his temptations, deceptions and lies. The only "mind games" that Satan has over a born again believer are the "mind games" that he or she allows him, he is a crafty sly devil (no pun intended) and is patiently waiting for you to let your guard down, then, he will ponce on you like there's no tomorrow (1 Peter 5:8 Be sober in spirit, be on the alert, "Your adversary, the devil, prowls around like a roaring lion, seeking who he may devour."

So, what do we do when the Tempter is tempting us, deceiving us and lying to us, how can we get him out of minds?

Let us learn from the Master Himself --
As we see in the book of Matthew chapter 4 when Satan was tempting Jesus in the wilderness, Jesus used the Scriptures to stop Satan's mind games. In all three of Satan's temptations, Jesus said "It is written", then He continues to quote Scriptures. Satan has no defense against the Word of God. James 4:7 "Submit" (to submit to God means having a relationship with Him through prayer and meditating on His Word) "therefore to God. Resist the devil and he will flee from you."

Sometimes, we need a bouncer at the door of our mind!!

Romans 12:2 "And do not be conformed to this world but be transformed by the renewing of your mind" (saturate your mind with the Word of God and become Satan's biggest fear), "so that you may prove what is that good, and acceptable, and perfect, will of God."

My daughter, Kathleen, and her husband, Jeff, are expecting their first child sometimes in August. Neither one of them wants to know what it is. Well, I thought that I would be the thoughtful caring grandfather type that I am, and suggest some Bible names right out of the good book of Romans chapter 16. Here are some for starters--

Sistah Phoebe, Aquila, Epaenetus, Adronicus, Junias, Ampliatus, Urbanus... Find one that you like? How about these... Apelles, Aristobulus, Herodion, Narcissus, Tryphaena, Tryphosa, Persis, Rufus, Asyncritus... Am I getting close? Try these... Phlegon, Hermes, Patrobas, Hermas, Philologus, Nereus, Olympas, Lucius, Sosipater, Erastus and Quartus.

I really hope that this helps you out, if not, you can stick with the more traditional names like Kathleenabus, Jeffreyicus or Davidoso.

Today's inventions will be tomorrow's antiques,
Today's youth will be tomorrow's elderly,
But, there is One who is the same yesterday, today and forever.

Do you know Him???

Father God, help me not to be "luke warm" with my life while I serve you on this earth, but rather, let me be HOT as the Texas sun in the middle of August.

If it weren't for the resurrection, Christ's death on the cross would be in vain.

SUPERNATURAL:
God wants to give His Super to your natural.

God can take your biggest mess into a message.

Though Jesus was resurrected from the dead one time, we should never stop celebrating.

Overcomer or Overcome?

Are you an overcomer, or, are you overcome?

-- 1 John 5:4-5 "For whoever is born of God overcomes the world. And this is the victory that has overcome the world -- OUR FAITH. Who is he who overcomes the world, but he who believes that the Jesus is the Son of God?"

Overcomers are followers of Christ who successfully resist the power and temptations of the world's system. An overcomer is not without sin, but holds on to his/her faith in Christ until the end. He does not turn away when times get tough and seem too hard to handle. Overcoming requires COMPLETE dependence upon God for His direction, purpose, fulfillment and strength to follow His plan for our lives. He has given us His sufficient grace to get us through those tough times.

-- 2 Corinthians 12:9 "But He said to me, "My grace is sufficient for you, for My power is made perfect in weakness.""

The Greek word most often translated "overcomer" stems from the word "Nike" (sound familiar?) which, according to Strong's Concordance, means "to carry off the victory." The verb implies a battle. The Bible teaches Christians to recognize that the world is a battlefield, however, God never leaves us defenseless in the battle, He has given us His armor and every weapon that we need to defeat the enemy (Ephesians 6:11-17), BUT, the armor won't work if you don't put it on. Sometimes, all that it takes to overcome temptation is to stand firm on what you know is right and refuse to be dragged into it. An overcomer is one who resists sin no matter what lures Satan uses.

With God's help, there is NOTHING that you can't overcome!!!

To Kathleen, my baby girl, I love you!!!
To my two boys Josh and Ben... I love you!!!

You do what you can do and let God do what you can't.

Take me to the WELL that will never run dry.

Let the redeemed of the Lord say so!!

We are a work in progress!!

Ephesians 2:20 ..."Jesus Christ Himself being the chief cornerstone, in whom the whole building, being fitted together, grows into a holy temple in the Lord, in whom you are also being built together for a dwelling place of God in the Spirit."

God's Love will bridge the gap of the deepest valley.

Happiness does not come by pursuing happiness for yourself...
... Happiness comes by pursuing happiness for others.

22

David Kurt McClain

Acts 5:1 "But a man named Ananias, with his wife, Sapphira sold a piece of property, and KEPT BACK some of the Profit for himself..."

Have you "kept back" praise and worship due to God?

Hey fear, sorrow, discouragement and diseases... SHUT UP!!!!

Lord I need You, Oh how I need You, every hour I need You.

The power of the spoken Word of "I AM"

"In the beginning God created the heaven and the earth." Genesis 1:1

God spoke and the heavens and the earth appeared out of nothing, He spoke our very existence into place. I AM penned the 10 commandments with just His voice. Just before His arrest, Jesus and three of His Disciples were surrounded by the Roman soldiers when they asked

"Which one of you is Jesus?" Jesus answered "I AM", and immediately the soldiers fell back. At the sound of His voice, the demons shutter and obey His every command.

Well, SIENNA GRACE landed last night safe and sound, actually, I'm not so sure about the sound part. It is official, I am a brand new Papaw. I want to thank each and every one of you who wrote a word of "Congrats" to my family and me – THANK YOU!!! There were so many of you that you used up all of my computer memory and my computer crashed... Lol... Really!!! I am the most blessed man on the face of the earth... Thank you Jesus!!! Not only has He given me years to see my daughter graduate college and all three of my kids get

134

married, now, He is allowing me to be part of my grandkids' lives. Bring on the grandcritters!!! 3-4-15

I want to take a moment or two to thank all ya'll who wished me a Happy Birthday and who congratulated me for the birth of my granddaughter SIENNA GRACE, it was a great day... THANK YOU!!!

Cool Your Engines and Say a Little Prayer

-- Matthew 5:44 "But I say to you, love your enemies and pray for those who persecute you..."

Me: "SAY WHAT??" Jesus: "What Don't You Understand??" Me: "You mean I am to love and pray for those who are mean to me and who hate me?" Jesus: "That's What I Said!" Me: "But my Lord, they talk behind my back, do I still pray for them?" Jesus: "Yes!" Me: "But my Lord, she hurt my feelings, do I pray for her?" Jesus: "Yes!" Me: "But my Lord, he is a back stabber, do I pray for him?" Jesus: "Yes!" Me: "But my Lord, I cannot do it by myself!" Jesus: "My son... That Is Why I Am Here!!!"

Many years ago, before I was ill with ALS, I would travel for the company that I worked for. On this particular day, I was in the airport terminal waiting to board the plane and suddenly I heard this man yelling and swearing on his cell phone. I remember thinking that this dude was extremely rude and inconsiderate. When we boarded the plane, he continued to be rude to the stewardess. By now, my blood was boiling and I was going to give him a piece of my mind once the plane landed. When the plane landed, he immediately got on his phone. I was going to wait for him in the terminal. As I was sliding out of my seat, I overheard his saying that he had just lost his son in a car accident. Immediately, my heart sank and I felt so ashamed for the attitude that I had towards him. This man was mourning his son and

135

was having a very hard time with it. Instead of a piece of my mind, this man needed a hug. I learned a valuable lesson that day. So many people are hurting inside and don't know how to handle it. You just never know if someone is lashing out because they are hurting. The next time that someone crosses you, before you retaliate by taking your shoe off and beating them with it, step back, take a deep breath, cool your engines, and say a little prayer. "If that doesn't work, then, take your shoe off and beat them with it"... Jk. Always remember "A soft answer turns away wrath" (Proverbs 15:1). When you are in a confrontation with someone, ask them how can you pray for them, either they will run away from you, or, they will open up to you.

-- Matthew 5:10-11 "Blessed are those who have been persecuted for the sake of righteousness, for theirs is the kingdom of heaven. Blessed are you when people insult you and persecute you... Rejoice and be glad, for great is your reward in heaven."

And on that day when my strength is failing,
The end draws near and my time has come,
Still my soul will sing Your praise unending,
Ten thousand years and then forever more.
(Matt Redman-10,000 Reasons)

I am not a great man of God, I am a man with a Great God.

Walk in the Spirit

Ever since Adam disobeyed God and sinned in the Garden of Eden, there has been an ongoing battle between our Spirit and our flesh.

Romans 5:12 "Therefore, just as through one man sin entered into the world, and death through sin, and so death spread to all men, because all have sinned."

The flesh will take all it can and can all it takes. The Spirit will enable you to walk the walk and talk the talk. -- Galatians 5:25 "If we live by the Spirit, let us also walk in the Spirit."

Galatians 5:16, 17, 24 "But I say, walk by the Spirit, and you will not carry out the desire of the flesh. For the flesh sets its desire against the Spirit, and the Spirit against the flesh; for these are in opposition to one another, so that you may not do the things that you please. Now those who belong to Christ Jesus have crucified the flesh with its passions and desires."

There is coming a day when we, as believers, will experience His command first hand. This is one day that I ain't going to miss!

Okay, here is the setting; all of the nations of the world and their armies come together one last time in an attempt to overthrow Jesus and His army (which is us who are believers. Now, this is the part that has me extremely excited, we will be riding behind Jesus on white horses, must be the Texan in me!).

Now, let's go to the text;
Revelation 19:11-16 "And I saw heaven opened, and Behold, a white horse, and He who sat on it is called Faithfull and True, and in righteousness He judges and wages war" (it's about to get good). "His eyes are a flame of fire, and on His head are many diadems; and He has a name written on Him which no one knows except Himself. He is clothed with a robe dipped in blood, and His name is called The Word of God. And the armies which are in heaven" (that's us), "clothed in fine linen, white and clean, were following Him on white horses" (YEEEHAW). "From His mouth came a sharp sword" (the sword is the spoken Word), "so that with it He may strike down the

nations" (how awesome is that? With just His Words, Jesus will slay the armies of the world. I wonder if Jesus will shout "I AM"), "and He will rule them with a rod of iron; and He treads the wine press of the fierce wrath of God, the Almighty. And on His robe and on His thigh He has a name written, "KING OF KINGS, and LORD OF LORDS." (Whow... can I get a witnessa!?!?)

PRESS ON!!!!!

You don't get good to get God,
You get God to get good.

The answers to your problems are in the Bible, not in the bottle.

Is your life in pieces? Allow God to PEACE it back together again.

The SON That Never Sets

While I was walking on the beach, one summer's eve,
I was engulfed with the warm feeling, of the summer breeze.
As I gazed upon the water, I saw a fisherman tending his net,
but, what caught my eye the most, was the magnificent sunset.
Golden yellow, brilliant orange and fiery red all pressed into one,
I had never seen such beauty, coming from the setting sun.

Immediately, I thought of the Creator, and my hands I did raise,
and joined in with the sun, to give the Father praise.
Got my worship on, and in the Spirit I will stay,
and then the sun slowly disappeared, only to rise another day.
Darkness chases the sunset, but, there's coming a time,
when darkness will cease to exist because of SONshine.

Because of the SONrise, we have won the fight,
sent by the Father to bring this of dark world light.
He brings strength to my soul and peace to my heart,
His mercy, grace and love for me will never depart.
Forgiver, Redeemer and Healer all pressed into one,
You are El Shaddai, Adonai, God's only Son.

Born to you die to rise, He paid our debt,
Jesus is our Savior and the SON that never sets.

By David K. McClain
5-12-15

No Compromise!!!

Don't worry about tomorrow, take care of today, then, go fishin'.

Stuck on a decision and can't decide on which way to go? Have you consulted with the One who knows you inside and out and knows what your needs are?

Psalm 32:8 "I will instruct you and teach you in the way you should go; I will guide you with My eye."

I won't stop until I cross the finish line!!

PRAISE ADONAI!!!
From the rising of the sun until the end of every day... Praise ADONAI!!!

ADONAI: The name means "Master" or "Lord". God, our Adonai, calls for all of God's people to acknowledge themselves as His servants, claiming His right to reign as Lord of our lives.

2 Samuel 7:18-20

Hope is raining down on me!!!!

Don't let your yesterday affect your tomorrow.

Let the weak say "I AM STRONG!!"
– Joel 3:10

WARNING: Not having Jesus Christ as your Lord and Savior WILL not only be hazardous to your health, but, WILL be eternally fatal to your soul.

Romans 10:9 "If you confess with your mouth that Jesus is Lord and believe in your heart that God has raised Him from the dead, you will be saved."

Deuteronomy 30:19b "So choose life in order that you may live, you and your descendants, by loving the Lord your God, by obeying His voice, and by holding fast to Him..."

To all of my Brotha's out there, this is my challenge to you... "Be The Man That God Wants You To Be!"

1 Corinthians 16:13 "Watch, stand fast in the faith, be brave, be strong" (no Retreat, no Compromise). Let all that you do be done with love.

Take this world but give me Jesus!!

Set Goals

So, there you are, compound bow in hand, loaded with your sharpest arrow. As you draw back the bowstring and release the arrow, you realize that there is a big problem... there is no target (hate when that happens!!). The arrow travels aimlessly through the air until force stops and gravity takes over. In a way, that's how life is without goals, aimlessly going through life that with no direction or target. It is NEVER too late to set goals.

Philippians 3:16 "I press toward the goal for the prize of the upward call of God in Christ Jesus."

Hypothetical Question

IF God spent as much time getting to know you as you spend getting to know Him, God is?...
(A) a total stranger
(B) a frequent flyer
(C) your best friend
or
(D) none of the above

Sometimes Jesus will calm the storm and other times He will calm the child going through the storm

In The Furnace

If a Potter were to never put his creation in the furnace, it would not be complete and could not be used. Sometimes, God will allow us, His creation, to go through the furnace in order to be complete, lacking in nothing (James 1:2-4). Also God will put us through the furnace to toughen our skin and strengthen our faith so we can be better used by God fulfilling His will for our lives. And remember, we are never in the furnace alone, just ask Shadrach, Meshach and Abednego. (Daniel chapter 3)

The answer to every problem that you will ever face in your lifetime, is found in the Word of God.

The Light will let you see, the Truth (Jesus) will set you free!!

The Light will let you see...
John 8:12 "Then Jesus again spoke to them, saying, "I am the light of the world. He who follows Me shall not walk in darkness, but have the light of life."

"The Truth will set you free..."
John 14:6 Jesus said to him, "I am the Way, and the TRUTH, and the Life, no one comes to the Father except through Me."

Got a craving for manna biscuits, fried catfish and blackberry cobbler.
Exodus 16:4 "Then the Lord said to Moses, "Behold, I will rain bread (manna) from heaven for you..."

If you seek Me, you will find Me.
Yeshua (Salvation)

Hellen Keller (blind and mute), was once asked "What could possibly be worse than being blind and mute?" Her reply... "Having sight but no vision!"

Proverbs 29:18 "Where there is no vision, the people will perish

Lord my Lord Jesus, Thank You for life's trials and lessons that bring us closer to You

The answer to the age old question:

Deuteronomy 30:19 "I call heaven and earth to witness against you today, that I have set before you, life and death, the blessing and the curse. SO CHOOSE LIFE in order that you may live, you and your descendants, by loving the Lord your God, by obeying His voice, by holding fast to Him..."

You can't know that which you don't believe in.
John 3:16 "For God so loved the world, that He gave His only begotten Son, that whosoever will BELIEVE in Him, will not perish, but, will have everlasting life."
No belief... No Jesus,
Know Jesus and you will most definitely believe.

What you are going through is not bigger than God.

I live for the King in His Kingdom.

I am the property of my Lord and Savior Jesus Christ, "Satan, what part of NO TRESPASSING don't you understand!?!?."

Lesson From God and the Silversmith

When a Silversmith makes pure silver, he must first start with impure silver. He will place the impure silver bars, coins, jewelry etc. into the vat and bring it to a boil. As the silver boils, the impurities, or dross, floats to the top. As the dross floats to the top, the Silversmith will "skim" it off and discard it. This process will go on until there is no more dross that floats to the top. The silversmith knows that it is pure silver when he can see his reflection in the vat.

Often times, God will allow us to experience different trials and testings in order to purge the "dross" and impurities out of our lives. James 1:2-6 "My Brethren, count it all joy when you fall into various trials, knowing that the testing of you faith produces patience. But let patience have it's perfect work, that you may be perfect and complete, lacking nothing. If any of you lacks wisdom, let him ask of God" (It's just that simple), "who gives to all liverally and without reproach and will be given to him. But let him ask in faith..."

When God allows us to go through trials and testings, it is not to punish us, but, rather to increase our faith in Him and to totally rely on Him and trust Him to get us through each and every trial... in other words...God has our back. When God looks into the vat of our lives, he wants to see His replection through our lives.

Instead of asking God... "Why me?", try asking..."Why not me?" Your trials are MUCH bigger than yourself, give God the reins of your trials and sit back and watch Him work wonders and miracles through you. Philippians 4:13 "I can do all things through Christ who strengthens me."

Luke 19:39-40 Some of the Pharisees in the crowd said to Him, "Teacher rebuke your disciples." But Jesus answered, "I tell you, if these become silent, the stones will cry out!"

If we become silent in our testimonies and praise, the stones will cry out and worship Him. What'll you say, let's give the stones the day off and give God our very best praise and worship.

Not Easy – But Worth It!

God never said that it would be easy, He only said that it will be worth it.

Matthew 5:10 "Blessed are those who have been persecuted for righteousness sake, for there is the Kingdom of heaven."

I have always been a positive and optimistic person, however, that wasn't the case 5 years ago. I had grown very tired and weary of living a motionless life. I had slipped into a very deep depression, I had given up hope and had to look up to see the bottom. In my head I started listening to the whispers and the lies of the enemy. Satan has one goal and one goal only... To destroy you and me. If it had not of been for the grace of God, your prayers and the living Word of God, he might have succeeded with me. Never let Satan rob you of your dreams and visions. When Jesus was tempted by Satan in the wilderness, He countered Satan's temptations with the Scriptures, leaving Satan completely defenseless. That is a lesson that we could all learn from the Master Teacher Himself, I certainly did. Jesus had totally changed my attitude and outlook on life by reminding me that my life was not mine to take, I belong to Him. He promised me that if I would totally surrender to Him, that He would bless me beyond measure. Since then, I have been able to watch my daughter graduate college, watch all three of my kids get married, wheel my daughter down the aisle, became a Papaw to two beautiful granddaughters via Ben and Mimi and Jeff and Kathleen, and a McBaby due in December via Josh and Ashley. My quiver is filling up fast. In his final speech, the great Lou Gehrig stated that he was the most blessed man on the face of the earth, he has now passed the baton off to me. Thanks to the ice bucket challenge, I truly believe that a treatment, then cure is right around the corner, I fully expect to be healed, if not by the wisdom of man, by the touch of God. I have my dancing boots polished and ready.

Jesus is the Lord of the way I feel!!

Give and it will be given unto you.

You Are

You were before were was
You are because are is
You are forever because forever will be
You are the Word and the Word is You
You are the light before light was
You are the rainbows' living colors
You are the flame that lights the wick in my soul
You are the Trinity... Father, Son, and Holy Spirit
You are Three in One... Equal and Eternal
You are the One who restores my soul
You are the One who bottles all of my tears and places them in Your Book
You are Jehovah Jireh... my Provider
You are Jehovah Rapha... my Healer
You are Beautiful
You are the Rock... Solid and never moving
You are All Knowing... All Powerful and everywhere at the same time
You are the Holy of Holies... the Bright and Morning Star
You are Peace... Faithfulness... Kindness... Gentleness... Goodness...
Joy... Patience & Awesome
You are the King of Kings and the Lord of Lords
You are God
You are my God!!
I just wish that I had the words that would have adequately described You.

By David K. McClain

Psalm 29:1-2
"Give unto the Lord, O you mighty ones,
Give unto the Lord glory and strength.
Give unto the Lord glory due His name,
worship the Lord in the beauty of holiness."

Psalm 29:11
"The Lord will give strength to His people.
The Lord will bless His people with peace."

Sounds like a pretty good trade off to me!

Tomorrow morning, when you are at church, close your eyes and let every word of the worship song or hymn speak to your heart, and when the preaching starts, open your eyes.

Change Friends

If disappointment is your closest friend, it is time to change friends.

Disappointment is one of those emotions that can lead us to bad places in our heads if we let it fester. There are Bible verses that remind us that we all have disappointments and others that shows us how to overcome the feelings of disappointment and keep our eyes on God's plan for our lives.

Romans 5:1-5 "Therefore, having been justified by faith, we have peace with God through our Lord Jesus Christ, through whom also we have access by faith into this grace in which we stand and rejoice in the hope of the glory of God. And not only that, but we also glory in tribulations, knowing that tribulation produces perseverance; and perseverance, character; and character."

"Hope. Now hope DOES NOT DISAPPOINT because the love of God has been poured out in our hearts by the Holy Spirit who was given to us."

Make Jesus your closest friend and He will turn your disappointment into hope and praise... Believe me, I know!!

Battle With The Gnats: The Next Chapter

First of all, I want to thank Stephanie Hill for recommending apple vinegar and dish soap... It works!!! However, there was one gnat who didn't get the memo to meet at the pool of death. Before I go on, let me go back one year. To shield my face from the gnats at night, Donna had bought one of those mesh screen tent thingy's that you see at picnics covering the bar b que, baked beans, or fruit salad. Anyway, so there I was, sleeping with this "food tent" over my head just to keep one tiny gnat away, but there's just one problem, the gnat snuck into the tent with my face and melon head. It was about to be a long night. As the gnat was checking out my skin preparing for its feast, I was figuring out my counter attack. It didn't take me long to realize that I had no counter attack. Now, I have never been water boarded, but having a gnat walking on your forehead has to be a close second. After about ten minutes, I was ready to give up our military secrets. I kept trying to scrunch up my nose hoping to crush it between my forehead wrinkles. As the gnat was canvasing what must have seemed like acres of skin, it was paying very close attention to my eyebrows, possibly for nesting and all kinds of breeding. Like I need a herd of gnats mating in my eyebrows. I knew that I had to act fast so I pulled out my old Cub Scout survivor guide. I had to build a trap or snare, because I had limited resources, all I had was my mouth, so, opened it, I did, and sho nuff, it only took 32 minutes for the gnat to find inner peace in my mouth. When all else fails... eat your enemy!!

Gnats my story and I'm sticking with it.

God is more interested with your finish, than with your start.

Happiness is circumstantial, but, the joy of Lord is constant and eternal.

Don't Fall for Satan's Placebo!

Placebo: a simulated or otherwise medically ineffectual treatment for a disease or other medical condition intended to DECEIVE THE RECIPIENT. (Wikipedia)

Satan is a liar and deceiver and spends his time trying to DECEIVE your heart with his lies.

When God created the earth, it was perfect. Then, God created Adam and Eve, giving them the 'title' to the earth. That's when the Deceiver set his snare and lured them in with his lies (he has that same snare set for you... always be equipped with the Sword of the Lord... Ephesians 6). Because Adam took the bait hook, line and sinker, he screwed it up for all of us.

Romans 5:12 "Therefore, just as through one man (Adam) sin entered into the world, and death through sin, and so death spread to all men" (way to go Adam!!!!)...

The very moment that Adam sinned against God in the Garden of Eden, he forfeited the rights to the title to Satan who became the god of this world.

-2 Corinthians 4:4 "In whose case the god of this world has blinded the minds of the unbelieving so that they might not see the light of the gospel of the glory of Christ, who is the image of God."

Often times, God gets a 'bad rap' and is blamed when bad things happen. Let's get one thing clear right up front, God is not the author of bad things in our life, that's just another lie straight out of Satan's playbook. Satan hates everything and everybody that God created, and that includes you and me. The reason that we have wars, famine, sickness, diseases and death, the reason that bad things happens to good people, the reason why kids get cancer, the reason why over

50% of marriage's end up in divorce, etc. etc. etc., is a direct effect of Satan's scheme to disrupt and destroy all that God has created. This left God with a temporary dilemma, how could a righteous, perfect holy God fellowship and commune with that which is not righteous, perfect and holy?... Answer --HE CAN'T!!! Satan is the author of sin and the wages of sin is death, God knew that because of our sin, we were a doomed people. Out of His love for all mankind, He sent His Son (John 3:16) to take on Himself every one of our sins and was nailed on the cross and died in our place. Each and every one of us was/are guilty of sin in the eyes of God. When Jesus died, He took our guilty sentence and nailed it to the cross. We are made righteous only through the shed blood of Jesus and can enter through heavens gates into the arms of God Himself. It is only by the grace of God that we can be saved from hell and have eternal life through our faith in Jesus Christ.

Ephesians 2:8 "For by grace you have been saved through faith, and that not of yourself" (there is absolutely nothing that we can do to work our way into heaven, Jesus did it all!), "it is the gift of God."

Satan still has access to heaven where he spends his time accusing you of your past before God. There is soon coming a day when Jesus will come back to reclaim the title to the earth and deal with Satan once and for all. "The next time Satan reminds you of your past, just remind him of his future!!" Carman

Revelation 20:10 "The devil, who deceived them, was cast into the lake of fire and all brimstone where the beast and the false prophet are also; and they will be tormented day and night forever and ever."

When we cross over to the other side, we will understand the whys of it all. Until then, keep pressing on!!

2 Corinthians 4:16-18 "Therefore we do not lose heart, but though the outer man is decaying, yet our inner man is being renewed day by day. For MOMENTARY, light affliction is producing for us an eternal weight of glory far beyond all comparison, while we look not at the things which are seen, but at the things which are not seen; for the things which are seen are temporal, but the things which are not seen are eternal."

In the end it will be understood, stay in the fight!!!

Need It or Want It?

Many times, God will give us what we need, rather than what we want.

Numbers 11:4-7 "The rabble (trouble makers) who were among them had greedy desires; and also the sons of Israel wept AGAIN and said, "Who will give us meat to eat? We remember the fish which we used to eat free in Egypt, the cucumbers and the melons and the leeks and the onions and the garlic, but now our appetite is gone. There is nothing to look at except this manna. Now the manna was like coriander seed, and its appearance like that of bdellium." (consisted of water soluble gum, a resin and an essential oil, used in perfume, as incense and as traditional medicine. It is more costly than myrrh and has a cluster of raisins look in appearance).

While the Israelite's were sick and tired of manna tasty cakes, they were craving "surf and turf" complaining when they didn't get it. God knew exactly what they needed and was providing their every need. How many times do we pray for something, then, complain when God doesn't answer our prayers exactly how we think that they should be answered. Just remember, God's ways are not our ways. If God looks after the sparrow in the field and meets its needs, what makes us think that God won't meet our needs, "... are we not greater than the sparrow?" Matthew 10:31

There is no distance in prayer.

God is in the house.

Manage your time wisely... or... Satan will!!
"You love the world and you're avoiding Me"
~~~Keith Green~~~
"I want you here with Me
but, you've been keeping other company
you can't sit still, it's plain to see
you love the world and <u>you're avoiding Me</u>"

There is a battle going on right now between you and the god of this world (Satan) over your time. The biggest threat to Satan is the saint who is actively involved in daily prayer, the reading and meditating on God's Word and being an ongoing witness for Jesus Christ by the way you live your life. You see, Satan knows that your greatest asset is your time and he knows that if he can fill up your time with "stuff" that you will no longer be a threat to him. Don't get 'stuffed' out of your relationship with God. You only have this very moment once in your life... spend it wisely and make it count.

If the shoe fits, wear it. If it doesn't fit, it's probably not your shoe!!

You reproduce what you are.

One Prayer Away

Nothing that we can say or do, there is nothing that we can bring,
to get us through heavens gates, except by the grace of God we cling.
Not by works or attending church, I know that sounds odd,
but by faith in Jesus Christ and by the grace of God.
So if you're feeling down and blue and fearful of that day,
through Christ, death is dead and salvation is one prayer away.

By David K. McClain

Jesus is my God-Father

Don't Sweat the Stuff

Don't sweat the small stuff, or, the large stuff for that matter!!

Years ago, before I became ill with ALS, I took for granted just about everything... Things like looking at the stars, watching the sun rise and set, the smell of Duncan Donuts dark roast coffee (when I had a tracheotomy, I lost 90% of my ability to smell), eating biscuits with creamed gravy, the feel of the warm summer's breeze on my face and telling those who I love that I love them.

Now, the small things are huge to me... Things like looking out my window, getting shaved, having my arms and legs lifted when they are stiff, having a massage twice each week, the feeling of a warm kiss on my forehead, or my face, or, for the chosen few, my lips... lol.

I DO NOT tell you this for you to feel sorry for me, I tell you this to encourage you to thank the Good Lord for your health, your God given abilities, and the special people that He has placed in your life. As for me, I am doing great, my faith in Jesus Christ has sustained me spiritually, mentally, emotionally and in His timing, physically.
Happy Thanksgiving!!

It won't work if it's not turned on, so is the same with you, get turned on to Jesus!!

The LAMB of GOD is in our midst!!!

Are you feeling down and blue this time of year? Has your praise and worship become stagnant? Has the excitement of being born again grown cold?

If so, it is time to make the spiritual 911 call!!

Psalm (91:1) "He who dwells in the secret place of the Most High shall abide under the shadow of the Almighty."

If at first you don't succeed, skydiving is not for you!!

We can see the signs, wonders and the beauty of God through His creation.

This Christmas Season let's make our Invisible God visible through His love and our actions.

It is far better to be the least of the least on this earth and have Jesus than to be the most of the most and not have Him as Lord of your life.

Psalm 84:10 "For a day in Your courts is better than a thousand. I would rather be a doorkeeper in the house of my God than dwell in the tents of wickedness." (the world).

"For though we are in the world, we are not of the world."

"But one of elders said to me, "Do not weep, Behold, the Lion of the tribe of Judah, the Root of David, has prevailed to open the scroll and to loose its seven seals."
Revelation 5:5

"You can take my heart out of Texas, but you can't take Texas out of my heart!"

David K. McClain
12-13-2015

Leigha singing 'Noel' to Papaw. 12-25-15

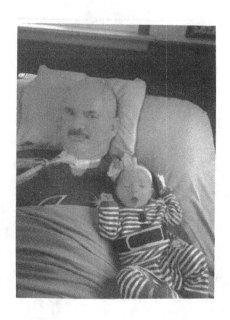

What If?

What if God hadn't sent His Son as Savior of this earth,
there'd be no star, no manger, no virgin birth.
There'd be no cross at Calvary, no life for Him to give,
no life eternal, no reason to live.
But, God loved this world so much that He DID send His Son,
His reason was to give the gift of salvation to everyone.
So, as this season brings you gifts and presents that you love,
let's not forget the Greatest Gift, sent from above.

DKM
12-29-2015

I have a feeling and am believing that 2016 will bring my healing.

12-30-2015

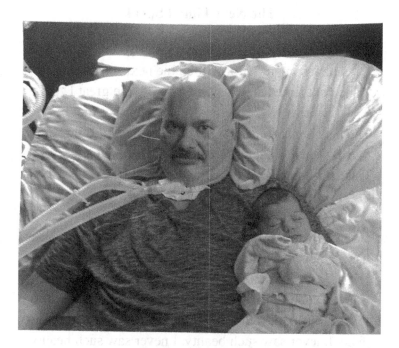

Papaw with Shiloh

Papaw with Sienna

The Next Time I Speak

The next time I speak, I'll say "Jesus You're my King",
a new song to Him, will be the next song I sing.
The next time I stand, will be before the great I AM,
my arms will raise up, to Gods perfect Lamb.
The next sunrise I see, will be the Son who rose for me.
I'll see His radiant face, and I'll live in His glory.
The next breath I take, could very well be my last, then,
I'll live eternally, and my sorrows will be past.

I want to run to Your embrace, I want to gaze into Your
face, I never saw such beauty, I never saw such beauty
sit here at Your table, I am just so grateful, I've never
known such freedom, I've never known such freedom
I want to run to Your embrace, I want to gaze into Your
face, I never saw such beauty, I never saw such beauty
and sit here at Your table, I am just so grateful, I've never
known such freedom, I've never known such freedom
I've never known, I've never known such, freedom.

The next time I speak, I'll say "Jesus You're my King",
a new song to him, will be the next song I sing.

The song's
First verse written by David K. McClain
Second verse written by Emily Vescovi
Composed and sang by Emily Vescovi

1/22/2011

Just My Shell

Be not upset, this is just my shell,
For I am free from death's grip and am doing well.
I currently stand before my King, where I will forever worship Him
and sing.
My earthly possessions remain on this ground, only my works done
for Christ
Shall I receive a crown.
Jesus took on death's sting when He hung on that tree,
He suffered, bled and died because He loves you and me.
He rose from the grave on that glorious third day,
And proclaims to the world that He is the Truth and the Way.
He knocks on your heart and extends out His hand,
He wants to save you, please let Him come in.
Accept Christ as Savior, friend you must decide,
Do not delay, do not deny!
As a result, I am saved from eternity in hell,
My home is now Heaven where forever I'll dwell.
Heaven is perfect, free of heartache and sin,
Free of pain and sickness, I am healed from within.
I am now in His glory, there will be no more tears,
I will be with my loved ones for eternity, not years.
There cometh a day when your journey too, shall end,
And all Heaven will rejoice when you are ushered in.
So, be not upset, but rejoice with me,
Death just starts life for eternity.

By David K. McClain

I am truly honored and blessed to be under the care of some of the finest doctors, nurses, and CNA's in the country. You have gone above and beyond in your care for me. It has been a privilege to experience first hand your skill and dedication that you practice towards your patients. You all have been such an important part of my life through this journey. Thank you for your special calling.

Dr. Raxlen's Letter

I have been one of the physicians privileged in helping Mr. McClain since 2004

During the period of his intractable ALS he has been able to communicate with the world through the ingenious invention of eye movement computer assisted spelling and speech laboriously moving his eyes over a TV monitor screen letter by letter. He is able to spell out words and turn them into "computer speech", produce written material blogs, shared personal thoughts even poems.

He is converting some of his writings record of his trials. I asked if I could share my personal thoughts about his remarkable story.

I first met Mr. David McClain, in July 2004. He was a robust father of three, married to his wife Donna for 25 years. He was employed as a steel manager for a steel company.

His initial symptoms were slurred speech, joint pain (hips, shoulders, toes) tired jaw cramping in throat (difficult to sing), and trouble swallowing.

He received a tick bite two years before he had visited me on his right thigh and a second tick bite 1 year later. He had seen a number of specialist physicians and had had electrocardiography which proved negative.

On examination his right eye was in able to focus only laterally, and he showed glossed pharyngeal nerve weakness with a deviation of his tongue. The right thumb and first fingers showed weak strength and his overall grip was weak. Other symptoms included testicular pain, lower abdominal pain, and an inability to power enough air to blow his nose.

With David's history of tick exposure, and his neurological symptoms following within 24 months a diagnosis of neuroborreliosis with bulbar involvement was made clinically by myself, and confirmed by Dr. Katz a neurologist in Connecticut familiar with the condition David was exhibiting. He was placed on IV antibiotics therapy and immediately responded in a positive manner. He reported more energy and was able to go to the gym to work out, breathing had improved. At night there was decreased drooling and he was able to blow his nose.

The diploplia had disappeared and there was no indication of any more hip pain and minimal joint pain.

In addition there were no more night sweats and there were no problems with leg cramping. This improvement was reported on 2/15/05, after 8 months upon completing I.V. antibiotics therapy on 5/11/05. Mr. McClain was feeling well enough to travel again for the steel company and was doing a remarkable 100 push-ups daily.

Fast forward to April 2016.

In spite of what appeared to be a remission after the IV antibiotic therapy, his medical condition took a turn for the worst and in a relatively short time following his improvement in 2005 he went rapidly downhill and went from wheelchair to being completely bed ridden.

As he has described so poignantly.

"I lay motionless for 23 of the 24 hours each day.
I am a prisoner in my own body, and alive mind in a dead shell. I cannot speak, eat or drink.
Swallowing is very difficult for me. I am fed by a feeding tube.
I have a hole in my neck, with a tracheotomy so I can breathe.
I am on a ventilator 24 hours 1 day. I cannot cough up secretions, I need a special machine to vacuum out my lungs.
My jaws will lock up causing me to bite my tongue. I have to buzz for someone to pry my jaw open.
My life is lived in my mind, I lay in bed with just my thoughts and memories"
The highlight of my day is when I am sleeping at night. When I dream at night I am not paralyzed.
I have a special computer that enables me to type, speak, and go on the internet with just the movement of my eyes.
I am totally dependent on machine and other people, just to survive each day.

You would think that someone in this incomprehensible, debilitation brutal situation would be seriously depressed, suicidal, crushed in spirit, aggrieved and hateful, furious at the world and above all a confirmed atheist, absolutely denying the existence of GOD, Christianity, the Holy Spirit and Jesus Christ.

Incredibly, this is not David McClain's feelings. In fact, it is the exact opposite. David McClain is an outstanding example of a man whose spiritual growth and evolution is disproportionate to his imprisoned physical deterioration. In my experience he without a doubt is the most spiritually evolved and faith sustained human being that I have had the privilege to know, either as a patient or in my own relationships.

The unassailable Christian faith of David McClain in his own articulate words:

"As I travel this journey through the "Shadow of death", fear is NOT an option, my Savior and my King, Jesus Christ has carried me this far and will continue to carry me until that day that he calls me home to Glory. The weaker I become physically, the stronger I become spiritually, this "raggedy old "corruptible" body will someday he "incorruptible". This mortal body will put on immortality, then "death will be swallowed by victory.

How great is that?!
In this world full of hatred, sadness and despair, there is a blessed hope through Jesus Christ that heaven is a "reality". Imagine a place where there will be no more tears, no more sorrow no more crying, and no more pain.
A place where earthly bodies will be transformed into glorified bodies, just like Jesus Christ when he rose from the grave.
It is a place where we will encounter loved ones and family and friends who have gone before and after us.
We will live in Christ's radiant glory for ever and ever. Trust your heart and your life to him to be the love of your life.

I offer you this challenge. Regardless of how high the mountains seem to be before you, or how deep the valleys may appear. Whatever the heavy weights that pull you down or the worries that drown your mind, know that his love is there. Give it over to Him!!!! Rejoice with me. Death just brings life eternal.

SEE YOU ON THE OTHER SIDE.!"

David McClain soldiers on despite his debilitating physical handicaps. His mind is constantly active communicating his thoughts in e-mails, blogs facebook page, and in computer driven speech.
His courageous example of endurance is an inspiration to his friends and family. All that is made possible in a large part, by the care giving support and love showered on him by his wife Donna and his three devoted children.

Donna has nursed him through his medical ordeal from the very beginning of his illness. She was with him at his first visit to my office and has stood by him throughout his 12 years illness.

Whether it be handling emergencies with the failure of his respirator or emergency suctioning of his trachea or maintaining his hygiene or bathing him (with the help of devoted aide), or even getting him ready for a special outside event at his daughter's graduation in a special van donated by caring friends.

His children Josh 29/ Ben 27/ Kathleen 24 are a great strength, responsible for many his needs. It is through them that he is last refreshed by their lives, and the outside world.

The poignant relationship with his children is written in a poem entitled *"Daddy Read to me."*

"Daddy please read to me, I love to hear your voice, stories from the bible are stories of my choice.

Daddy please sit next to me, let me hold your hand.
Daddy don't leave me, please read to me again."

Then comes David's debilitating illness which has left him speechless and paralyzed, so the song poignantly shifts.

I lay in my bed immobile, imprisoned in my sheets,
Terminally sick, I cannot speak, my days I cannot tell.
My arms and my legs are paralyzed, alive throughout the day
When she walks by, and she can hear me say
"Kathleen please read to me, I love to hear your voice,
Stories from the bible are stories of my choice.
Kathleen please sit next to me, let me hold your hand.
Kathleen don't leave me, please read to me again."

Life is but a vapor, soon I will go home

Then Kathleen I will read to you
Yes, you will hear my voice
I will sit next to you and I will hold your hand
I will never leave you
We are in the Promised Land

The song beautifully expresses the juxtaposition of a father's strength and his unconditional love, and his child's unshakable trust. Then their dramatically change as the father is struck down and the child becomes the strength bonded with unconditional love and the father becomes the helpless child-like trusting dependent.

The psychoanalytic author Michael Eigen has written extensively about faith and psychoanalytic experience in his illuminating book "Faith".

"There are dimensions in our lives in which faith, mystical experience, and catastrophe are part of the human experience."

The question is, what can faith do in situations where there is no control, no way out?

It is one of the mysteries of faith that at time of catastrophe it helps us sit with, suffer, endure and grow through such life situations.

A striking expression of faith is Job's (biblical) ordeal. "He cries out to the Lord" though You slay me, yet I will trust You."

"Another ultimate moment is when Abraham on the mountain willing to obey yet love God by the sacrifice of his only son Isaac."

In answer to Isaac's question, "Where is the animal sacrifice," Abraham's answer is an answer of faith. "God will provide the lamb, my son."

Or the faith of the "suffering, Jesus" on the cross crying out "Father why have You forsaken me."

In the face of death there is faith. Even in the face of heart-breaking loss of faith, there is faith." – Unbreakable Faith

Faith that is rooted in profound grace, deeper than catastrophe that transcends survival and earthly sorrow and loss. It is through faith we hear the heartbeat of the world, of basic existence.

Mr. David McClain and his children are remarkable in their continued devotion in the face of the enormous task for caring for David's survival.

In the difficult times when the task may have appeared to overwhelm them, it was David's pure, unbroken faith that sustained them all.

This remarkable man has survived 12 years. 10 years longer than the medical outcome predictions would approximate.

He has evolved spiritually, and in many ways has transcended his physical prison.

The "dead shell", that he refers to as his mortal body has brought forth a faith, so profound and inspiring, that one can only stands in awe of the life force and the empowering spirituality that it generates. He survives because of his Christian faith.
He is transcendent.

Profoundest respect,
Dr. Raxlen

Dr. Takoudes's Letter

I first met David McClain while he was admitted to Gaylord Hospital, a terrific center in Wallingford, CT, that focuses on caring for patients with illnesses that require long term specialty care. He had just had a tracheotomy tube placement because his ALS had progressed to the point where he was starting to require mechanical ventilation. This is a difficult time for people with ALS as it signifies progression of the disease to a point where their ability to breathe and live now becomes entirely dependent on a machine as your diaphragm muscle fails.

There are two special facets of caring for David that have really stuck out with me. The first is that I have gotten to know him so well despite the fact that he has never spoken a word to me or written me a note. His courage and determination are unmistakable. When we meet (always in the setting of my performing a procedure on him) I see the gleam in his eye and his subtle smile, which are his way of showing me he is tackling every day with a will to do whatever he can to continue on. No fear, no hesitation, just an enthusiastic charge forward to treat his illness.

The second is David's relationship with his wonderful wife, Donna. Donna decided early on in David's illness that she would learn how to care for him and provide high level nursing and respiratory care that has kept David healthy in a way that I have never seen. Caring for a patient with a tracheotomy requires diligence and a knowledge base that are difficult to master. Donna asked me, the nurses, the respiratory therapists, really the entire medical team, as many questions as she needed to truly understand how to best care for David. For the first few years of my caring for David, Donna and I had several lengthy conversations reviewing the ins and outs of advanced tracheotomy care. She has mastered tracheotomy and ventilator management. I have cared for many long-term ventilator dependent patients. Most eventually succumb to their illness as the lungs become weak and damaged because of the imperfections that exist when a ventilator takes over the body's breathing function. Not David. He has demonstrated a longevity and good health that is unparalleled because of the terrific care he has received from his wife.

I am proud to know David and Donna. They have tackled David's ALS with courage, enthusiasm, diligence and a quest to master complicated medical care and medical equipment in a way that has extended David's lifespan and improved his quality of life in an immeasurable way. I am sure his story will offer the wisdom and inspiration that I have seen time and time again over the years while caring for him. -Thomas G. Takoudes, MD, Otolaryngologist - Head and Neck Surgeon, March 2016.

Dr. Rodrigues's Letter

To David and Donna,

I consider it a unique privilege to have been involved in your lives.

Despite the degree of physical challenges that David has endured, it did not change his greeting. I was always welcomed with a wide smile, and that smile reflected his spirit and strength.

I remember clearly a conversation with Donna outside David's ICU room when he was just placed on mechanical ventilation. She said that their kids needed their father growing up and she was going to make sure that he would be there for them. It seemed like a false sense of bravado at that time, but they have put together a phenomenal run. When I visit their home and see pictures of David at the kids' weddings, and now the grandchildren, they look to me like trophies of a race well run.

It's truly been an enriching experience for me as a person as well as a physician. Having managed an intensive care unit for many years, I can fully appreciate the meticulous attention to detail and resolve that it has taken to allow this miracle to go on.

You two are an inspiration.

Allan Rodrigues

Dr. Metzger's Letter

March 2016

We have had the pleasure of knowing David McClain for about 9 years since he was a patient in my office. As his condition progressed I began treating him in his home for the past 5 years. As any doctor can tell you, we treat a variety of different complaints and people tend to complain about the most common ailments. However, Dave does not fit that category by any stretch of the imagination!! When I visit him in his home he is always smiling with his eyes and when I ask him "Dave, what is bothering you today?" He will respond on his eye scanner that he is "doing good today, and everything is fine!". This is coming from a man who cannot move any muscle in his body except his eyes! His positive outlook and amazing attitude can only come from a source higher than himself, namely His Lord and Savior, Jesus Christ. I appreciate David and his example of persevering through tremendous trials everyday and he encourages me to appreciate each day that God gives us.

James M. Metzger, DC, CCSP

February 13, 2012

David McClain
68 Roosevelt Street Ext.
New Haven, CT 06513

Dear David,

Not long ago I received word from your college friend Laura Rutter about you and your situation and I immediately thought, "I wish I could sit down and talk face-to-face." You see, I've also had to struggle through the "ups and downs" of physical problems due to a paralyzing injury from a diving accident more than 40 years ago. I've learned to appreciate the power of encouragement—a personal letter with a verse from God's Word, a sensitive message cheering me on, etc.

And that's what this letter is meant to be. When your day-to-day routine seems, at best, boring, when the tiniest of tasks seems overwhelming, when you feel knocked down one too many times, when you face the pressure of meeting other's expectations, please know that you're not alone. There are others (me included) who daily face the same problems, the same routines. And we have found that God can come through in a powerful and personal way to give strength and hope.

It's like the verse says from Psalm 73:26, 28, "My health fails; my spirits droop, yet God remains! He is the strength of my heart; He is mine forever!... I get as close to Him as I can!"

So thanks for spending a few moments with me through this letter, David. And please know we will be praying for you. If there's one thing for certain, we can pray with empathy and understanding. Thank you for trusting the Lord Jesus even when it's difficult. May God bless you for that!

Thanks for listening,

Joni Eareckson Tada

Enes.

David Kurt McClain

To: texupnorth@msn.com
Date: Wed, 20 Jul 2011 13:41:58 -0500
Subject: Thank you

David,

Thank you for being the person that you are. Your attitude and strength are amazing. You are truly an inspiration to us all. The entire Dallas Cowboys family and I appreciate your support.

Best, Jason Garrett

My son, Ben, had the opportunity to share his testimony as well as my letter with the Baltimore Ravens after connecting with one of their former players, O.J. Brigance. He also has ALS and continues to be an inspiration to the team.

ATTITUDE

*"The longer I live, the more I realize the
impact of attitude on life. Attitude, to me,
is more important than facts.*

––––––––––

*It is more important than the past, than
education, than money, than circumstances, than
failures, than successes, than what other people
think or say or do. It is more important than
appearance, giftedness, or skill. It will make or
break a company . . . a church . . . a home.*

––––––––––

*The remarkable thing is we have a choice every
day regarding the attitude we will embrace
for that day. We cannot change our past . . .
we cannot change the fact that people will act in
a certain way. We cannot change the inevitable.
The only thing we can do is play on the one
string we have, and that is our attitude . . .*

––––––––––

*I am convinced that life is 10% what happens to
me and 90% how I react to it. And so it is with
you . . . we are in charge of our Attitudes."*

– CHARLES SWINDOLL –

ODE TO DAVID WITH ALS

3-2-07
Grace McClain

You gave him desire to sing,
But took away his voice;
You gave him talent to draw,
But can no longer hold a pen-
You gave him words to say,
Then took away his speech.
You gave him strength to build,
though now his strength is gone
"Blessed is the name of the Lord"
You gave him grace today –
"The Lord gives & takes away"
Now You alone are his strength.
You alone his stay.
He no longer builds with wood.
He builds with silver & gold
As You are building his Mansion –
Too beautiful to behold –
His inner man renews
Though his outer man decays
As he waits to sing with angels
His great Redeemer's praise!

When the Time is Right

Words and Music by Matthew Ouellette

Written for David McClain

I know it's not what you dreamed it'd be
A song you never thought you'd sing
A road you've never known
A story not your own
A day you never thought you'd see

I know that you had different plans
A life that's held in other hands
Altered mountain heights
Changing form of fights
The nights that you had hoped to dance

But you're standing taller than you ever could
You're speaking louder that you ever would
Your light is brightest in the darkest night
Your faith is stronger in the greater fight
I'll take you home when the time is right

You've come to know sufficient grace
You've felt My love in a thousand ways
Peace to you I give
It's My life you live
In My story you're My page

But you're standing taller than you ever could
You're speaking louder than you ever would
Your light is brightest in the darkest night
Your faith is stronger in the greater fight
I'll take you home when the time is right

But you're standing taller than you ever could
You're speaking louder than you ever would
Your light is brightest in the darkest night
Your faith is stronger in the greater fight
I'll take you home when the time is right

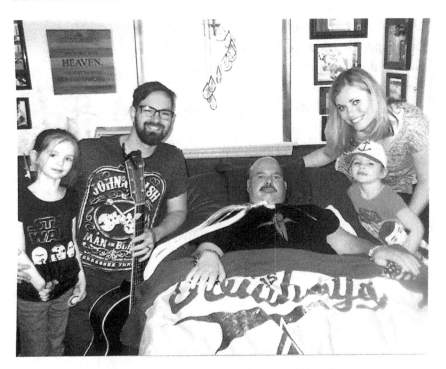

Macy, Matthew, Me, Missy, and Presley
(April 2016)

I am without words to express my gratitude and thanks to Matthew and his Family. Not only did he write a song for me, but he and his family drove down from Maine and he sang it to me. He also gave to me a copy of his book, <u>Thoughts that fell from a TACO SHELL.</u>

Thanks, I love you guys!

David K. McClain's
e-mail

Texupnorth@msn.com

Printed in the United States
By Bookmasters